OUR HEROES NEXT DOOR

Helen O. Bigelow

Our Heroes Next Door

WORLD WAR II MEMORIES REVEALED BY VETERANS

Helen O. Bigelow

Copyright © 2022 by Helen O. Bigelow

All rights reserved. No part of this book may be reproduced in any manner whatsoever without written permission except in the case of brief quotations embodied in critical articles and reviews.

First Printing, 2022

Book Cover Design by the Book Cover Whisperer: OpenBookDesign.biz

Contents

Acknowledgements	1
Preface	2

THE VETERANS — 3

1	Donald Dick ~ Looking the Enemy in the Eye	4
2	Bruce Sherman ~ Storms Caught Us Going and Coming	8
3	Joseph Ambriz ~ The Beer Was In The Hold	13
4	Gerald Johnston ~ The Germans Greeted Us At Normandy	15
5	Robert Goodrich ~ The Japanese Occupy Many Islands	19
6	Evelyn Yonka ~ The WACs Go To North Africa	21
7	Joseph Burzynski ~ I Was A Stevedore	25
8	William Burgess ~ We Shared Hot Saké	27
9	Edwin Robert Main ~ Okinawa Was A Hotspot	31
10	Olaf Rose ~ New Caledonia Was Our Base	34
11	Wilbur Cook ~ We Were The Guinea Pigs	38

vi | Contents

12 William Meadowcroft ~ My Brother Was Killed In France — 41

13 John Burder ~ Dirtiest Ship In The Fleet — 44

14 Rufus Camp ~ Japanese Pilots 15 Years Old — 48

15 Ernest Rabineau ~ Talking To The Queen Of England — 51

16 Calvin Winters ~ I Wanted In The Army — 55

17 Donald Steiner ~ Two Kamikazi Planes Came: We Got Them — 58

18 Bill Cheolas ~ The Gliders Came In First — 63

19 Charles Carson ~ Sandblasting With Ground Walnut Shells — 68

20 Heinz Anger ~ Fighting In Hitler's Army — 73

21 Emerson Kennedy ~ Dodging Submarines In The Pacific — 77

22 Edward Swartz ~ Three Of My Ships Sank — 81

23 Burney James (Jim) Elliott ~ We Get Even With The Army — 84

24 Anonymous ~ Dual Citizenship Becomes A Problem — 87

25 Andrew Duke ~ Guarding At The Hospital — 92

26 Arthur Morton Fishman ~ Military Acknowledges My Jewish Heritage — 94

27 Cornelia Fort ~ The Arizona Went Down — 98

THE ROSIES — 101

28 Beulah McAlister — 102

Contents | *vii*

29	Dorothy Martus	104
30	Elizabeth (Betty) McInally	106

OTHER WAR EFFORTS 109

31	A Jewish Voice For Veterans ~ A Veteran's Voice For Jews	110
32	Tuskegee Airmen	112
33	Japanese Americans in World War II Combat	114
34	Prisoner of War Camps in 1943	115
35	War Brings Changes At Home	119
36	Author's World War II Memories	121

Appreciation from Veterans Esteem Team	127
About The Author	129

Acknowledgements

Many thanks to the World War II veterans who opened up their past to give us their stories even though it was difficult at times. Some enlisted while others were drafted, but all served their country.

Many women served in the military branches such as the WACs, WAVEs, WASPs, and SPARs. Other women worked as Rosies in jobs replacing men who had gone into the military.

Thanks to the Koning family for making me aware of many veterans, for those who provided transportation to interviews, to Yvonne Brown for helping me to get my book published, and to those who helped me with support in any way to accomplish this project.

Preface

World War II Veterans Reunion, 2021
Brown City, Michigan

The World War II veterans you will meet on these pages stepped out of their homes and entered into a life of heartbreak, danger, loneliness, and fear of death beyond any we can imagine. Many lost contact with their families for months at a time. We, here at home, did not know where they were and could only pray, write, and worry about them, hoping they were safe. It was a difficult time, and there is no way we can thank them enough for keeping the enemy away from our shores. It is a time we can never forget and hope to never repeat.

The persons and places mentioned are included to the best of the veterans' recollections. Any misrepresentations are unintentional.

THE VETERANS

World War II Memorial, Washington, DC.

1

Donald Dick ~ Looking the Enemy in the Eye

I am Donald Dick, and I am 98 years old. I was 18 years old when I joined the Army Air Corps. Boot camp was in Miami Beach, Florida. From there I went to Denver School of Armament where I learned a lot about guns. In Panama City, Florida, my wings were pinned on me and I learned how to be a gunner on planes. Back in South Carolina I practiced with pilots as I would have to do in combat.

When I got to Italy – no more practicing. We flew missions regularly. My pilot liked me, treated me like a son. We became lifelong friends. He had me at the guns right behind his back.

I was stationed in North Africa first. The Germans came in and bombed the base, destroying it. We then flew out of a base on the island of Corsica just south of Italy.

Axis Sally was a trained propagandist radio broadcaster from Maine in the U.S.A. She knew what was going on and where. She kept the German Army informed of where to attack. She was given credit for the airfield destruction in North Africa and other places. After all, the German Army had hired her to do that – besides talking on the radio to try to get in the minds of our men. The Corsicans treated us good but didn't like the Italians. Some Italians came over and took jobs away from the Corsicans. The Corsicans were a more backward people.

Our 487th squadron had a big shot, Dr. Kindahl. He was a famous man and did a lot for us. He was good to me and knew my voice if I was around. He brought in whiskey and saw to it that each man had some when we came in from a mission.

We had a little setback again when Mt. Etna erupted and destroyed our airfield and everything on it. Sally was given credit for that too and many other things.

At one time, I had two carrier pigeons to care for. We had them to carry emergency messages if we had no radio.

We destroyed many bridges, highways, trains, and towers to interrupt transportation and communication. Many things we did affected the citizens too, for houses and public buildings like schools and stores were destroyed. All of this affects the person we become by remembering it later. On one trip returning over water from France, a young man jumped out of the back of the plane. Another behind him realized he was making a mistake but had gone too far to turn back and completed his jump. We looked for them but couldn't find them.

We went to Italy for R & R (rest and relaxation). Italy has some beautiful women, and it is a beautiful country.

One Sunday morning a young girl in the drug store followed me around for two days. I took her to dinner and said, "Good-bye". I always wondered what happened to her. We always carried things like candy and gum to give to the kids.

Black airmen loaded our bombs to be brought to Corsica and then Blacks unloaded them on Corsica. There were no Black pilots until the Tuskegee Squadron was formed in Alabama. The military also did not have women in combat.

On one flight, a German fighter plane pulled up close beside us. I was in the gunner's position and could look that German pilot right in the eyes. I will never forget those eyes. However, his little prank didn't end the way he'd planned. As he sped away, I shot his plane. I don't know if I got him, but stuff was coming out of the back of the plane.

A trip I always hated was when the aqueduct was our target. We destroyed some of it. This city had no electricity and depended on that aqueduct to bring their water down from the mountains. I flew seventy missions and sometimes I felt bad about what we did – like destroying the aqueduct.

I went home on leave, arriving tired at the bus station. I was READY to be home. A stranger came up to me and asked where my family lived. He told me they didn't live there anymore. He took me to their new home.

After my two weeks leave, I was sent to gunnery training in California for a year. Then I went for more training in Panama City, Florida, where I stayed until the war ended. When I was discharged, they asked if I wanted to join the reserves. I said, "No!". Finally, I figured it was safe now that we weren't at war, so I joined the reserves.

Then came the Korean War and 400 of us were called back into service. I flew night missions in a B29 program for a year or more. After that war I was sent home. I, again, signed up in the reserves. Some of my training was in New Mexico during the Korean War. Then I went home for good after being in the service for seventeen and a half years.

I worked at Pontiac Motors, retiring from there with a pension. I stay busy going to military meetings and carving. I've made many carvings. Some are as tall as ten or twelve feet.

I got married while I was at Selfridge Airfield, and we have five children.

2

Bruce Sherman ~ Storms Caught Us Going and Coming

I am Bruce Sherman, and I was born in Cass City, Michigan, in 1927. There were thirteen of us, six girls and seven boys. My dad was a farmer, so we had no trouble keeping us all busy.

Before I was drafted, I hauled 160 eighty-pound cans of milk each day to the dairy. I was only seventeen years old.

After I was drafted, I was sent to the Aberdeen Proving Grounds in Maryland for Basic Training. There I went to school for wheel and vehicle mechanics.

We went to Pittsburg, California, where we were boarded on a ship for the Philippine Islands. Going the northern route, as we neared the Aleutian Islands, our ship broke down. It took a week to get it repaired.

I had a great surprise when we reached the Philippines. There on the dock was my brother to greet me. He was stationed about three miles from me there on the island, so we saw each other often during the few weeks we were both there.

I was glad we had landed, for on the way over I had to cook every other day. I learned some good recipes and a lot about cooking.

In the Philippines, I had charge of quite a large repair business. There were five bays with two vehicles in each bay. I had twenty-five Filipinos working for me, and we were all kept pretty busy.

From there, they put me in a Jeep shop as an inspector. I inspected each Jeep and wrote up orders for what repairs were needed. I did that for ten months. Then I had to release the work done to the owner. I was a Buck Private. An officer came around and saw what I was doing. He said what I was doing was not a Buck Private's paying job. He sent me to CQ – Charge Quarters – where I checked in the rifles of those coming off guard duty. My rate now was T-5.

One night a man wanted to enter the camp who was not in uniform. I didn't give him a pass. If he had entered without a uniform, he would have been shot soon. He wasn't happy that I didn't give him a pass, and he blew out my candle leaving me in the dark. We were having transformer problems and were without electricity. If he had gone downtown, he would have been anyone's game. It was a very dangerous place.

In Manila, Philippines, the war ended, but the fighting didn't. Guards were shot and later found a ways from the camp. Doubling guards on duty helped the situation greatly.

We took a side trip over to the island of Corregidor which is in the Manila Bay area. This rocky, rough, mountainous island was very hard to take from the Japanese because of all the places to hide. We saw evidence of the fight in the number of empty cartridges that covered the roads. It must have been especially well-fortified for the largest barracks to exist were there.

When the war was over, many of us were being sent home. At sea on the way, we were caught in a terrific storm. Our anchor broke loose and knocked a hole in the front of the ship. We were at the mercy of the storm. For a week, we slept in our life jackets while the water came three feet deep over the deck. We finally landed back in San Francisco, California, and took a train to Fort Sheridan for discharge. I had served for two and a half years.

During the following years, I returned to the farm and worked at it while working other places too. I worked at the Packard Building making 2900-pound jet engines. I worked several places, always working on vehicles. The last place I worked was at Saginaw Steering Gear as a millwright.

I was the leader there, and every six months I got a new apprentice to be trained. My manager said I was the best millwright ever and the best that can come. He wanted to clone me!

I was married before I entered Army life. Our commander kept track of how often we wrote to our families. If we didn't write every week or two, he reminded us to do it. My wife and I had six children – three boys and three girls.

In the past I was a wild game hunter. Now, I just cook the holiday turkeys.

I am very active. I am head of the VFW Bingo program, official of the Cass City Dance Club, and Vice President of the Sandusky Dance Club. I love to dance. Another vet down the road and I go dancing every two weeks.

I am proud of the time when a milk truck was brought in one day where I was working, and the driver said it needed a new motor by 8:00 a.m. when he started his route. I had it done!

12 | HELEN O. BIGELOW

3

Joseph Ambriz ~ The Beer Was In The Hold

My name is Joseph Ambriz, and I was born in Detroit, Michigan. There were two girls and one boy in our family. My dad worked at the Ford Rouge plant in Dearborn, Michigan.

I was drafted into the Navy and went to boot camp at Great Lakes Camp in Chicago, Illinois. I was sent to San Pedro, California, where I stayed for ten months.

14 | HELEN O. BIGELOW

From there, I was sent to Hawaii. This was after the war so there was a lot of clean-up to do in all the islands. I had tugboat duty. There were many tugboats tied to buoys waiting to be loaded with supplies to be taken to many destinations. When they were taken into the docks, they were then sent to larger boats. One of the main items to be transferred was beer. The main destination for the beer was to the officers' clubs. Some didn't reach its destination for we broke open the cases, helped ourselves, and put it in the refrigerator we kept on our tugboat.

There were large barges that had sleeping quarters for us. They also cooked our food on the barges and brought it to us ready to eat. It was said that 70% of the food was thrown out because it was buggy. Some of the bugs were quite large.

Cat Houses were available on the island. They disappeared when the WACs and WAVES arrived on the island.

Since I was considered the old man of the unit, I was tagged with the nickname "Daddy Joe".

I was married three times. My first wife had bought the house where my son-in-law and I live now. We had three girls who now live in Redford and Southfield. I have three grandchildren and five great grandchildren. My second wife and I were divorced, and my third wife has died.

I still live near Lexington, Michigan, and stay busy even at 96 years old. We heat our small house with a pot-belly stove. I make six stacks of wood to last us through the winter.

I like to read Western stories. The old authors of Westerns are all gone, but I sometimes can find their books at yard sales.

I have belonged to the American Legion for 63 years.

4

Gerald Johnston ~ The Germans Greeted Us At Normandy

My name is Gerald Johnston, but I am usually called Jerry. I was born in Flint, Michigan, in 1925. My father was a farmer. I was one of five children. My parents wanted NO children, so he and my mother were mean to us, showing we were not loved. My father found a reason every day to beat us with a board. As a result, I left home when I was fourteen. I had worked at a pickle factory where they hired kids at any age and saved my money. I earned $22 per week. I bought an old Model A Ford, and a friend and I headed for Detroit. I stopped at the Coca-Cola factory and asked for a job. When they found out I was only fourteen, they sent me to a high school to get working papers. They hired me, and I worked there until one day I got an idea to ride the rails. My friend didn't like the idea but went along with me. That didn't last long for we were getting sparks of fire from the engine on our perch below the front car.

My friend left me in Ohio where I got a job as water boy in the circus. That lasted one day. I headed back to Detroit where at eighteen years I was drafted into the U.S. Army. Boot camp was in Fort Knox, Kentucky, where we did a lot of hiking and calisthenics for eighteen weeks. From there we went to Virginia where we boarded an LST to Europe. We encountered a lot of submarines on the way.

We were greeted in Normandy Beach with a barrage of shells, both large and small, coming at us from shore. Many didn't make it. Three of us were running side by side. I was shot in the back. I carry the shrapnel yet today. The other two men were killed. I was left for dead. When the guys came to pick up the dead, they saw me move a finger and said, "Heh, this one's still alive!" They sent me to a hospital and in a week I was back on a tank. This fighting in Normandy continued for two weeks.

Normandy Beach
National World War II Museum

I guess farm boys have the same qualifications as tank gunners for that's where they put me. I was inside the tank with the trigger on the floor controlled by my feet. The tanks were on the front lines of the battle. We encountered fierce battles with Germany. The first time our tank was disabled by the enemy we took heavy fire that went right through us and set us on fire. We had to scramble to escape out the trap door in the bottom of the tank between the tracks.

The second time the enemy fire left big cracks in our tank destroying it. Again, we scrambled to the trap door at the bottom of the tank.

The third time we were left inoperable our tracks were blown off the tank. New tanks were brought to the front line.

We met some Russians who were our allies at the time but didn't like us. They were busy in battle with the Germans.

We had both C rations and K rations. The K rations had three cigarettes and candy in them. The C rations had canned food, usually some hash which I didn't like and other food. Once in a while we had pork and beans. I liked that!

While walking in the woods, I heard a 50-caliber machine gun being racked. I looked up and met a German eye to eye. He didn't fire and neither did I.

I was taking a radio wire near where we knew the enemy was so our forces would know what was ahead for us. As I walked, I passed a German officer lying dead nearby. Looking over the knoll, I saw a whole battalion sitting by a bonfire, relaxing, probably after eating. Even though we knew they could come after us, we watched and did not kill them. The next day a truckload of kids (young new American recruits) appeared to help with the battle. They went up the hill to take on the enemy, and they were "sitting ducks" – making good targets for the Germans. Most were killed.

Just by hearing bits and pieces of their language every day, I learned enough German to get a lot of valuable information. I became the translator for the German POW's (prisoners of war) and translated their information to our officers.

We were all happy when D Day happened, and we knew we would be going home.

At home, I was able to find work at a foundry where I worked until I retired. I farmed along with my job. I was married and we had five children. I now live alone with help near Kingston, Michigan.

5

Robert Goodrich ~ The Japanese Occupy Many Islands

I, Robert Goodrich, was born in Sandusky, Michigan, in 1925. My dad was a printer at the Marlette Leader. My mom was not content to stay home, so she was usually working at a dress shop or some other small business in town.

I enlisted in the U.S. Army First Infantry Division. Boot camp was in Oregon where we did a lot of hiking and learned how to care for and use our rifles.

Basic training was in San Louie Obispo, California. Here we learned how to climb ropes up the side of the ship and descend quickly by doing it over and over. We were an invading group. I was in three invasions within five months. Then, we returned to the Philippines to await further orders. After the Japanese were driven out of the Philippine Islands, the Philippines became a sort of home base for many military branches and units.

Between invasions, we were an occupational force to relieve units on the small islands. The Navy and Air Corps had cleared the space before, so it was safe for us to go in. The enemy had been cleared out, so we didn't encounter any resistance to our occupation.

In Tokyo, the Japanese stayed hidden from us because they had heard stories about how Americans murdered their babies and attacked the people. Actually, we were just looking for a bar to get a cold beer.

We were in the hill country on Leyte when the war ended in 1945. When the news reached us, we didn't believe it.

General McArthur came to Leyte while we were there. The people (and we) hated him. There were stories about how he packed up his family, closed up his home, and left the Philippines to spend the duration of the war in Australia. This left his troops and the people there to the mercy of the Japanese. (People admitted the story was hearsay.)

One small island we were to occupy so the Marines could leave had been in a fierce battle with the Japanese the day before. It was reported that 70% of the Marines had been killed. When we arrived, the land, shore, and shallow water was littered with bodies. A big Marine came up to me and asked me, "Why are you worried? There are two ways to get off the islands – severely wounded or dead."

We saw Bob Hope in Hawaii. His one night of entertainment was a relief after our past experiences.

When I had been home on furlough in 1943, I dated my high school girlfriend and we got engaged. During the three years since, we had not spoken or seen each other. Soon after I arrived home, we were married. We had 69 years together. We had three daughters. At first, I worked in the printing office with my dad. Later, I was the purchasing agent in the mobile home industry until retirement here in Marlette. I would sure like to be in Florida though!

6

Evelyn Yonka ~ The WACs Go To North Africa

I, Evelyn Yonka, was born in St. Louis, Missouri, the oldest of six children. I had five brothers. My parents, Julianne and Martin Dunajcik, immigrated to the United States from Slovakia before I was born. My father was a blacksmith, and my mother was a good cook. I grew up in the Great Depression when food was scarce and expensive, so I was never allowed to cook.

Once the war broke out, my brothers, Walter and Albert, were drafted. My younger brothers, Eugene and Ralph later served in the Korean War. After her sons left, my mother said she was glad women were not being drafted, only to learn I was going to go too.

When the United States declared war on Japan in December of 1941 and then Germany and Italy declared war on the United States, the only American women in uniform were members of the Army Nurse Corps and Navy Nurse Corps. The other WAC members and I were the trail blazers who paved the way for others to join the military in World War II.

At first, WACs did not receive rank benefits or even pay equivalent to the men. In 1943, the Women's Auxiliary Corps became the Women's Army Corps (WAC) and were officially part of the U.S. Army. This entitled us to serve overseas and gave us more benefits.

After basic training, my WAC Army Air Corps unit was assigned to work overseas in Foggia, Italy, which was such a dirty place. This was partly due to air raids that left much of the residential districts, airports, and railroad stations devastated.

Getting there to Foggio was stressful because flying in the cargo section of a military plane overseas was frightening. It was also a noisy, bumpy ride. All we had to sit on were wooden benches.

It was where I went and the women of the WAC who shared my journey and remained my friends long after the war that I'll always remember. We had a grand time travelling together for training in New York and on assignment overseas. I was tickled to go to Italy because of the plays, arts, and music there. It also enabled me to travel. That was one of the perks I loved most.

At first, our duties were mostly clerical, but we were happy to be helping the war effort. Because of my business classes in high school, I was trained to be a teletype operator. Because of the ability to send messages fast, teletype machines became very important to the military. Other duties of the WAC were soon added, such as weather observers and forecasters, radio operators, cryptographers, parachute riggers, bomb sight maintenance, aerial photography analysts, and control tower operators.

One reason my work was interesting was because teletype operators never knew what sort of message or information we might receive. It could be coded messages having to do with strategic military action, or just news to be shared. One such message I received was about the famous band leader, Glenn Miller, who disappeared over the English Channel in a military plane.

The message that D Day had come – the war was over – came over the teletype. By then there were about 350,000 American women in uniform of which 150,000 were of the WAC. Though we did not serve in combat roles, 432 women were killed and 88 taken prisoner.

I loved my job. I am the last surviving member of my WAC HQ Plat 12 AF Unit.

It was interesting work.

My last day of service was September 15, 1945. I had served two years.

After the war, I married Mark Yonka, who worked with the military police. We had five children. I worked as a telephone operator and volunteered as a scout master. I retired at 65, and after my husband died, I returned to St. Louis to care for my handicapped brother.

I enjoyed travelling, but most of my trips were associated with anniversaries of military events or funerals.

On May 31, 2021, I was blessed with 100th birthday wishes, cards, and visits from many of my children, their spouses, grand and great grandchildren, nephews and nieces, friends, and cousins. I also received a 100th birthday letter from the National World War II Museum. My son, Terry, and my daughter, Mary, see that I am well cared for here in Michigan at the Sunrise Senior Living Home.

7

Joseph Burzynski ~ I Was A Stevedore

I, Joseph Burzynski, was born in Detroit, Michigan, in 1927. I have five brothers and one sister. My father was a building contractor and my mom cooked for big Polish weddings. One of my brothers was drafted into the Army.

I went to technical high school. I enlisted in the Navy at seventeen and was called in before I finished twelfth grade. I missed my graduation. Because of my high school background, I asked to be in a construction program. I was put into a Seabee Battalion.

I was first sent to Hawaii where I was trained as a lineman. Then I was shipped out to Okinawa. The old tug I was on broke down on the way. We were towed into Guam for repairs. When we arrived in Guam, we were told not to go beyond a certain point. They told us there were Japanese still there who didn't know the war had ended. They could come out and shoot us.

Some of the men stayed on Guam waiting to go to Okinawa after our ship was repaired. The rest of us flew on into Okinawa.

Not knowing what it was, I volunteered to be a stevedore. For six months, I helped load and unload supply ships.

The war had just ended, and we were no longer needed, so we waited for orders to be sent home. In the meantime, some men who had lower points and wouldn't be going home soon were issued fur-lined vests. We knew they were being sent to Korea. I had been in the Navy long enough to accumulate enough points to qualify me for discharge.

When I came home, I went to electronics school. I got married to the woman I spent sixty-five years with. We had four children.

My first job after electronics school was with Michigan Bell Telephone Company. I was a residential installer. After six years, I was installing thirty-line instruments. After I retired, I was freelancing for AT&T.

8

William Burgess ~ We Shared Hot Saké

My name is William Burgess. I was born in the hill country of Kentucky. There were five of us kids. I was the middle one.

My father didn't work. He was a moonshiner. My mom was in the bootlegging business. She had an apron with large pockets where she put her money. We weren't educated people but we knew how to soup up our cars so we could outrun the revenuers.

My father had been in the horse artillery in World War I. He sued the government and tried for years to get a pension before he finally got a small amount.

I went to country schools, finishing eighth grade. Of all the boys I knew, I was the only one who finished grade 8. Many never went to school at all. At one school where I went, there were two twenty-one-year-old boys in grades three and four. At sixteen, I got a job at a factory in Louisville that lasted until I was old enough for the draft.

When some of my friends and I were drafted in the Army, we were sent by train to Louisiana. We were at the Infantry Replacement Training Center. Most of us were southern guys who could neither read nor write, making an X for our names. The guys from the north made fun of those who couldn't read or write, and also made fun of those who had scars or welts on their backs from beatings. I read letters and wrote letters for the men. The northerners called it the marblehead college, poking fun at us. Some of the guys were content to just make the X.

There were five men in each of our plank-floored tents. In our tent was a husky, strong bully who caused a lot of fights. Almost everyone was afraid of him. Our six-foot four-inch man was afraid but schemed how to get the best of him. Finally, one day when the bully came at him, the tall guy hit him with his fist as hard as he could in the face. When the bully went down, his feet turned and his ankle broke. He went to the hospital. That was the end of the bullying!

In boot camp, I was learning about guns. This interested me so I bought a manual and learned a lot about different guns. This turned out to get me a lot of special work throughout my military career. For instance, I learned that the German rifle was superior to ours but ours could shoot twenty bullets in a flash.

We were at a disadvantage during the war for all our supplies, equipment, and vehicles (including tanks!) had to be shipped to the battle areas. I classified the German equipment as killing weapons while ours were wounding weapons. However, we had ways to get around some of the differences. We could come at the bigger, heavier German tanks with our lighter ones from two sides and destroy them. Sometimes their tracks came off. Our tank hunters were quite successful.

My oldest brother and our uncle went to basic training together. My uncle joined General Patton's Army, bringing up tanks to St. Lo. Our uncle was killed in that battle.

One of my brothers was a recruiting sergeant. He could not go overseas due to his lack of education.

I later learned the Japanese rifles had such long bayonets that they cut their fingers when trying to fire the guns. It was a much lighter rifle to carry than ours was though.

There was a ten-day delay in our next orders coming, so I went home. I got married.

Studying about the different rifles was so important. New ones were coming out – even a gas rifle. As my sergeant put it ... "There are two kinds of men – the quick ones and the dead ones".

Our new orders sent us to Mindanao in the Philippines. It was decided I was to be trained as a flame thrower, so I was sent back to Kansas. After training, I was sent to Seattle and boarded a big, old rusty ship headed for Japan. The war had ended, and all land areas were covered with debris. Trees were cut, hoping the rain would wash everything into the sea. Some Japanese were still hiding on the islands. They would come out to dig up graves to get the combat boots of the dead and slink back into the woods.

In Manilla, our captain saw Japanese still hiding in fox holes and the trees. They stayed in so long they were left behind.

Hiroshima was chosen as an atomic bomb target because the headquarters of their 6th Army was there. We got on a big ship and went there after the bomb was dropped. Everything was in ruin, lots of rubble and debris. We were warned that it was common for women to wear heavy, loose clothing to hide guns. We were told to be careful and watchful. We were left to patrol Yokohama. There we met Charlie. Charlie was unique. He spoke four languages. His big heavy coat had protected him from the effects of the bomb. We positioned ourselves so as not to shoot one another. Charlie's daughter brought out a tray of hot saké. As she passed it around, I took her drink and drank it. She knew why I did that, so she took my drink and drank it.

There were very few cars in Japan. There were fire boxes where fires had to be kept going to have power. We used three-wheeled cycles.

I could work with some of these Japanese because I had learned to understand and speak some of the language. That, again, got me some jobs others couldn't do. Sometimes I was called on as an interpreter.

On Honshu, engineers came in to load up unexploded bombs. They were taken to the Mariana Islands to dump them in the seven-mile-deep waters.

We left Yokohama and went to Shikoku Island. The Japanese had a community bath here that they used. We Americans used their two large pools. Women came out to towel us.

Some girls were made slaves at fifteen years old. They were taught languages so they could be interpreters. They were released at 25 years of age.

When it was time for me to be discharged, my wife met me in Louisville. I got a job in an antique machine shop. We raised our son and daughter there in Louisville.

My military records were burned, so I have received no benefits.

AUTHOR'S NOTE: I found Bill to be a very interesting person. He has such detail of events. He reads papers, books, or anything he can get about World War II.

9

Edwin Robert Main ~ Okinawa Was A Hotspot

I, Edwin Robert (Bob) Main, was born in Detroit. I had three brothers. Jack joined the Navy and Evart joined the Army. I enlisted in the Navy and was sent to boot camp at Great Lakes in Illinois. There we learned to march, be respectful, and listen.

In Norfolk, Virginia, I boarded the USS Strive. This was a minesweeper. Passing through the Panama Canal we headed for the Pacific

Ocean. We stopped first at Pearl Harbor, then headed for the South China Sea. The area around Okinawa was a popular spot for the Japanese to be actively laying mines, hoping to keep people away. So, we had to keep going back and sweeping the area. Our missions were especially dangerous because we had to go into an area first and sweep it for mines before any other unit could go there. Our sweepers were small ships that could get in closer to shore than larger ships could. If a Japanese plane appeared overhead, destroyers protected us.

Once a mine we were pulling in got tangled in our net. We couldn't pull it onto our ship, so we dragged it for one and a half days, trying to decide what to do with it and hoping it didn't explode. One day I stood there alone looking at the mine and trying to figure out what we could do with it. I finally asked for two men to tie a rope around my waist and hold on to me while I crawled down the cable. Using cutters, I cut the net and cable holding the mine and it floated away. That's one mine we didn't get. After that, I was promoted from First Class Seaman to Third Class Petty Officer.

A week later, back in the United States, my ship was sold, and I boarded a heavy cruiser for thirty days. This was just before the first atomic bomb was dropped on Japan.

I was discharged and went home. I got married, and we had a son and a daughter.

I wanted to farm but that career was cut short when I lost an arm in a corn picker accident.

My father-in-law and his cousin had adjoining properties. The cousin bought a small plane and made an air strip crossing both properties. When my father-in-law charged his cousin rent on the acres he was using of his, his cousin refused to pay. However, he kept using the air strip. My father-in-law told me if I could find a way to spoil the air strip, he would give me an acre to build a house on. I still had a tractor, so I hooked on to a piece of machinery and dug up a section of the air strip. I got the acre of land! The rest of the air strip was planted to trees.

I worked at Oakdale Center as General Supervisor until I retired.

I started a VFW unit in Otter Lake and was active with post military friends.

10

Olaf Rose ~ New Caledonia Was Our Base

I, Olaf Rose, was born in Massachusetts on August 15, 1921. I was drafted into the U.S. Navy in 1942 and sent to boot camp in Great Lakes in Chicago, Illinois. From there, all types of military branches were taken by train to President, California. There we met the crew ship that would take us to the island in the South Pacific that would be our base for a while, New Caledonia. This had been where rich

Japanese had lived with guarded fences. There also was a Japanese camp for those with leprosy.

Here we developed a crew and got our boat, PT171, with torpedoes and guns. The Japanese Army had occupied many islands in the South Pacific and our job was to take over the islands. We sailed in groups of five to seven ships. Groups varied in size, for sometimes if one of our ships was sunk or hit a stump or some other object, we would take on a ship from another larger group. Mother ships were at sea too where we could get supplies if we ran low. These supplies were from the U.S. and available in the Philippines also.

When we were in conflict with Japanese on an island, planes overhead helped us in the attack. Then the Army or Marines finished the job upon landing.

Each night we were back on New Caledonia. We weren't always safe there because of the snakes hanging from the trees. The Seabees set up camp for us and the Army was already there ahead of us, so when we came in each night, our group was not alone.

Going out each day we looked for large ships. With several PTs attacking, we were able to sink some. They were far out at sea, and we had to make sure we had enough gas to get back. It took 50 gallons. One tanker ship we sank was loaded with supplies for the Japanese.

Truck Island was rough terrain, full of caves. We knew the caves had Japanese and we couldn't get at them. We decided to leave them and starve them by cutting off their supply ships.

Tokyo Rose was on her phone constantly using her propaganda to antagonize our men. It was hard on the guys who had "Dear John" letters to hear their girlfriends were seeing other men at home while they were away fighting.

General MacArthur did a lot by driving the Japanese out of the Philippines. Many locals joined forces with him. President Truman fired him for not following orders.

The Air Corps picked up Japanese planes that were shot down, hoping to find information that might be useful to us. Suicide planes were commonly used by the Japanese to sink our big ships. Suicide was an honorable act by Japanese.

I saw Bob Hope several times – three times at Christmas. He was funny and, of course, we men all enjoyed seeing the pretty women.

Natives on New Caledonia and other islands liked us because we gave them candy, gum, and food. One gave me a big bunch of bananas. He had a big ring in his nose.

Now that the people back home had the atom bomb made and it had been delivered to Leyte, we knew we'd soon be going home. Two bombs had been dropped on Japanese cities. President Truman met Japanese officials on the USS Missouri and the peace deal was signed.

Soon I returned to the United States and was discharged. It was good to be back home with my wife, who I had married many months ago while home on leave.

Upon arriving home, we cut wood, let it dry for several months, and built our first home with no modern equipment or tools. In fact, we soon built a second home. We had a girl and a boy, so we needed a third bedroom.

We lived there in Crescent Lake, driving back and forth to the farm in Lapeer and working at Pontiac Motors for years. When both of my parents were gone, we moved to the house where I was born in 1988, and I am still here celebrating my 100th birthday.

Department of Justice. Office of the U.S. Attorney for the Northern Judicial District of California. NARA 296677.

AUTHOR'S NOTE: Tokyo Rose was found, arrested, and convicted of treason. She served six years in prison. President Ford then pardoned her. Her name was Iva Toguri d'Aquino.

11

Wilbur Cook ~ We Were The Guinea Pigs

My name is Wilbur Cook. I was born in Capac, Michigan, in 1925. My mother died the day I was born, and I was adopted by an uncle. The family name was Kampe, but I took my mother's maiden name. I was 19 when I enlisted in 1944. I had a farm deferment but enlisted anyway.

I went to the Air Corps boot camp in Wichita Falls, Texas. It was an Air Corps cadet training pilot program. Actually, it was a lot of drills and physical exercising.

Then we were sent to Randolph Field, Texas, to an aviators' school of medicine where we were used as guinea pigs. The flight surgeon used us for a lot of testing. We never knew what they were testing for or what they were using on us. We would fall out for roll call and they would point to us and say, "We want you, you, and you. Report to the aviation school of medicine for tests."

For motion sickness, there was a swing with a 90-degree angle that we sat in for an hour. If we didn't get sick, we passed. Once I ate little breakfast and got sick right away. They sent me for lunch and had me try again. On a full stomach, I passed. In fact, I did the best I ever had.

We were put in high altitude chambers, with altitudes higher than any plane could go at that time. They took vitals as we went up higher and higher. Oxygen was checked continuously (if you lost oxygen for four seconds you could pass out). Without oxygen they would count to ten. I saw no one who got past six without passing out. There is no physical sign you're out of oxygen – no headache, out of breath – nothing.

Another test we had was in a cold chamber. For this test, we had a different style of oxygen and wore oxygen masks. We wore electric-heated underwear. I was in this testing program for nine months.

After one year in service, I was promoted to Corporal and given two stripes, but everything else remained the same. At the end of the war, I was a staff car driver.

Then, I was sent to Enid, Oklahoma, where I trained for two weeks in basic mechanics. I was on a flightline maintenance crew. We gassed up planes, checked spark plugs, washed windows, etc. We had an A.M. flightline when we each had a plane to do a final check on before they flew. That included inside equipment like the radio. As the planes took off, we did a "fire watch", looking for anything that might look like a problem. While the planes were gone for three hours, we had free time. The next day it was all repeated.

The flight surgeons had to do interviews. They practiced on us.

At war's end, I had been in only 22 months of service. For discharge, there was a point system used. Those being in service longest were to be discharged first. But, since they didn't need our crew, they decided to take us first. They had us line up and sign a paper telling where we wanted to go to be discharged. I put Scottville, Illinois. I was second on the list. Shortly an orderly appeared and said he had two openings for Scottville. "Turn in all equipment except your dress uniform." I was out in 24 hours.

In leaving Scottville, I hitchhiked to Ohio State University to meet a girl. Then I hitchhiked home to Capac, Michigan, where I surprised my parents by walking up to them when they were at the mailbox.

Soon after I got home, I went to Michigan State University for four years, graduating with a degree in Agriculture Engineering. I worked for five or six years in the U.S. Department of Agriculture with the Soil Conservation Service. I stayed with them for nine years. It was during this time that I met a pretty girl from Ludington who later became my wife.

My father and I bought the local farm equipment dealership, and we worked at that for twenty-five years. Later I became a salesman for one of the suppliers we did business with.

After retirement, I sold G.M. autos for four or five years there in Marlette. Then it was time to retire again!

12

William Meadowcroft ~ My Brother Was Killed In France

My name is William Meadowcroft, and I was a Radioman First Class in the U.S. Navy. My family lived in Massachusetts. I had a brother twelve years my senior who was serving in the U.S. Army in Europe.

After being drafted at 19, I was sent to boot camp in Boston and was trained as a radioman. The top six men in training were sent for advanced training. Being second in my class, I was one of them. Later, I had even more training in Texas.

I was tops in receiving and sending messages, coding, and decoding. No one except the lieutenant and myself were allowed in the room where the coding machines were. Each location had its own four-letter code for receiving and sending messages.

One day a radioman stopped me and said he was sorry that my brother had been killed. I hadn't heard. I assumed it came over the radio. Later my father confirmed it. My brother was buried in France. Later his remains were moved to the United States.

I spent only three weeks on a ship. Then Guam was my home base. I always felt the reason I was not sent to sea again during the war was because my brother had been killed.

I felt very special when I travelled from California to Guam because I sat between a general and an admiral on the plane. The only other time I saw the admiral was during a hurricane on Guam. Hurrying to safety, many rushed into my room, including the admiral. Realizing they were in a restricted area, the admiral rushed everyone out.

I had a lot of free time on Guam. We played baseball. I was hit in the jaw with the ball. This required a lot of dental work and surgery. It seemed no matter what medicine he used, the doctor could not get the jaw healed. Finally, he told me he was going to try something new – with my permission. After using penicillin, my jaw was healed.

Another time while playing ball, my friend Jack, thought he had been stung on the side of his head. We saw blood and took him to the hospital. The doctor said he'd been shot. Soon the Japanese soldier who shot Jack came out of the woods to surrender. He didn't know the war had ended. Later more Japanese soldiers appeared.

Due to segregation practices at that time, I had no women or African Americans in my unit at any time.

I was in Guam when the war ended and was discharged at 21 years of age. I was home about ten days when I went back to school for five semesters. I graduated with a degree in civil engineering. I went to a job near Grand Rapids as a health engineer.

A friend told me Hillsdale needed a health engineer, so I went there for two years. About that time the federal government said if I didn't use it soon, I would lose my one year left on the G.I. educational benefits. I went and graduated as a sanitary engineer. I then worked as a public works director for five years and as city manager for ten years in Hillsdale. I retired at 62 and enjoyed life with my wife and two children.

13

John Burder ~ Dirtiest Ship In The Fleet

    I am John Burder. I was born in Pontiac, Michigan, in 1926. I had one brother. When I was 18, I enlisted in the U.S. Navy. Boot camp was at Great Lakes in Chicago, Illinois. Then I went to Norfolk, Virginia, for further training. There, day after day we went out for rides on ships to get acquainted with living and working on ships. I then was assigned to a crew on an LSM (Landing Ship Medium). An LSM had 54 sailors and five officers. Five hundred of these LSM's were made for moving supplies of any kind from one place to another. While we waited for our LSM to have its final painting, we loaded ships waiting to head for the South Pacific. Our LSM came out a dirty dark green color instead of the regular gray. We stood out midst other ships.

We left Norfolk via the Panama Canal and up, heading for San Diego and on to the South Pacific. As we sailed north, a sailor was brought to our LSM suffering with a serious appendix problem. It was more than we could handle so we pulled up near a Mexican town for help. Our rowboat was too small for transferring him, so we radioed into town for a larger boat to take him in. There was not a hospital nearby, so the local doctors did the surgery – asking for my assistance. I gave the sailor shots every two hours. He thought I was a medic. Then he was flown to the United States and we continued on to San Diego and eventually the Philippines.

From the Philippines, our main job was to get equipment and supplies to the islands closer to Japan. The Japanese hampered our work all they could. Their planes came as we worked but did not attack. Our boats had 898 guns firing at them.

When ships were anchored in the bays, we had to have guards protecting the ships at night for the Japanese kids tried to swim out to us. My turn at guard duty was a far cry from my job as a storekeeper. My job was to keep our store full. Sometimes we were able to get what we needed in the Philippines. We were in and out of there a lot. Sometimes supplies were transferred in big nets from other ships at sea.

I was called to do other duties often. One time I steered our ship for three days. This was done in the lower part of the boat near the kitchen. I enjoyed smelling the food cooking, especially the bread baking.

If a ship was hit or had problems, our LSMs were sent out to tow them into the Philippines for repair. We pulled along side of them and attached them to our LSM with a heavy cable.

When we left the ship and were on the islands, the locals wanted to buy things from us, especially cigarettes. One sailor sold all his packs of cigarettes, filled the empty box with toilet tissue, and sold it. When the angry man came back, I had to get out my .45 to get rid of him.

One time the captain said I had a job – hiding the beer he was bringing aboard – 40 cases! After hard days at sea, the men were given a bottle of beer after dinner.

Another job I got was paying the seamen. In all the time I was in the South Pacific I was paid only three times.

General MacArthur came ashore. People started taking his picture. He asked that they be taken over from a different angle because he didn't like that dirty green LSM in the background.

We missed our families when we were out to sea since we couldn't send or get letters.

My rate of pay and classification changed often. Both changed because your job determined both. I changed jobs temporarily often. I was promoted twice within a month, so my classification and rate of pay changed each time.

Our ship's compass went on the fritz when we were at sea. We were in constant touch with a nearby ship and used their compass readings to get back to bay. There was an Army ship there in the bay. Their head man offered to help me get a local man who would help me find the part we needed. We walked and walked. I was afraid of the man. We were gone some time and I was hungry. We came to a tent where a man was cooking. My companion said to grab a tray and help myself. I looked at the strange food and decided I wasn't that hungry. The captain didn't give up on me, and he didn't leave without me.

The field hospital gave us a delivery order from the Army. There was no place to unload. We went to the far side of Fukok Island near Japan and were able to unload the Jeep, truck, and trailer there.

We needed a sewing machine. When we ordered, they sent two. The captain's wife tried sewing, but the captain's assistant used it the most. He made an outlandish blouse that everyone made fun of. The second machine was traded for a diving suit.

The atomic bombs destined for Japan were made in the U.S.A. and shipped to Leyte on the USS Indianapolis. After delivering the bombs, the Japanese sank the USS Indianapolis. The bombings soon brought the peace agreement. After that, all Flagstaff left early. Paperwork was not done, so no one got paid.

All Flagstaff were ordered to Guam to join another officer's group. That officer left for Hawaii. I was moved to an amphibious group where I was now moved to Second Class. At the end, there was a lot of shifting people around.

Many, many guns and other equipment and supplies the Japanese left on the islands were gathered up and dropped in the ocean.

Victory was celebrated in the Philippines with fireworks and a lot of cheering and hugs. We were still at sea among the islands. We made a long line of boats, 36 in all, and headed for the Philippines. From there, we were sent to Guam before heading home.

There is a Japanese submarine on Guam for the public to visit or kids to play on if they like.

Upon discharge, I signed up for four years in the reserves, thinking the war was over and I'd be home. Korea happened! I was called back to Korea and later Guam where I was to keep charge of all supplies coming and going to Guam.

I now live in Lapeer, Michigan.

14

Rufus Camp ~ Japanese Pilots 15 Years Old

Although most call me "Red", my name is Rufus Camp. I was born in Alma, Michigan, in 1926. There were seven children, five boys and two girls. Four of us boys were in the military, one in the Coast Guard, two in the Army, and I was in the Navy. I was in a long line of the recruiters when one called out that he needed another Navy. I was only sixteen years old, two months shy of the legal age, but they put me through.

OUR HEROES NEXT DOOR | 49

I was sent to Great Lakes boot camp where I learned to obey and keep my eyes and ears open. Then I was sent to Virginia and on to Europe. I spent one week in England learning how to operate and care for landing crafts. There were Marines with us during this training. Then we were sent back to Virginia where we left the Marines. Here, I graduated into an amphibious corp. I was head of ten men. The men were taught signals to use when landing in open battle and went down. At this time my role was that of a medic. If a man yelled that he was alive, I crossed his arms and checked for blood. Then I had to determine if he should go to the hospital or if I should take care of him. (I had medical training back in Virginia in a hospital.)

We had to take Marines to Iwo Jima. There were many big battles before the island was taken. The Japanese had dug large, long tunnels where they could stay well-hidden for long periods of time. It took many lives before our flag flew over Iwo Jima.

Going back and forth between the Philippines and Okinawa was risky. We were constantly attacked by Japanese planes. We were able to take some of the pilots as prisoners from those planes we shot down. During questioning them we found many to be only fifteen years old.

We sat for four hours waiting for the BIG bomb that was due that day. We were close enough to witness the mushroom, but far enough away to be safe. Now we'd be going home!

Before long, arrangements were made for the peace ceremony. It was to be in Tokyo Bay. The USS Missouri dropped anchor. It was time for the emperor to board. Having arrived on shore upon a white horse, he gave his sword to General MacArthur, got in his little Japanese dingy, and boarded the USS Missouri to sign the treaty. I witnessed all this up to this point. All the men in white on the ship and those of us who witnessed the history-making event, tossed our hats into the air and shouted.

It took some time before we would go home. During that period, we had to wait our turn depending on how many points we had accumulated. I got home in 1950. This time, right after the treaty was signed,

I was aboard ships loading and unloading equipment returning it from the Philippine Islands and other islands to the United States.

It was 1950, and I had no intentions of staying longer. I had had four years in the service, but after I got home, I got a call to go back and be upgraded in the SEALs. That was the new name for the amphibious group I had served in. I was in the SEALs for two years.

When I returned home, I was married, and we had three boys. They served – one in the Seabees and two in the Army.

Because of the end of the war causing changeovers to regular products, there was a time it was hard to find work in the auto factories. When that period ended, I found work at G.M. where I worked for twenty-four years when I retired.

Since that time, I have been busy – even at ninety-five! – going to food banks or farmers, or anyone who has excess food, and delivering it to the needy. I work at this five days a week.

15

Ernest Rabineau ~ Talking To The Queen Of England

I am Ernest Rabineau, born in a very poor family of fifteen children. We lived in the Upper Peninsula of Michigan where it got so cold in winter that we had inch-thick ice frozen on our windows.

In 1943, at eighteen years of age, I was drafted into the U.S. Army. Of the seven boys in our family, all of us were drafted in the war. My mother had seven blue stars hanging in her window. Amazingly, we all came home after the war, but two came home with injuries.

After being drafted, I was sent to boot camp in Fort Benning, Georgia.

I was then sent to England for several months. There I fell in love at first sight with Nancy who was from Wales. I first saw her as she watched me when I was in a parade. I found her later and we started dating. About the time we were getting serious, orders came that we were shipping out at 3:00 a.m. I never saw Nancy again.

At parade rest, the Queen of England and her husband stopped to talk to me. She asked how old I was. When I told her I was 18, she said she was 18 too. She was very pleasant and beautiful.

We then headed for Calais, France, where German pill boxes greeted us all along Normandy Beach. This whole area was in German control. At first, France was soft and wishy-washy about Hitler being in France. The French soon learned he was there to conquer. On our third day there, I saw my best friend fall. That was quite a jolt to me. He and I had been best friends since grade school and spent lots of time at each other's home.

We were equipped with a backpack and a rifle. Our sergeant lectured us, "You are in enemy territory. You will have maybe a second to decide if you will kill or be killed."

From there we took a train to Belgium. We were very glad to get out of France where the people were very unfriendly. The Belgians were happy to see us.

We were fortunate not to have to depend on C-rations all the time. Trucks with large tanks of hot soup kept us pretty well satisfied while we were in combat, for we could have all we wanted.

When they found out I knew Morse code, I was promoted to sergeant in the signal corps. A radio and binoculars were added to the gear I had to carry.

When our 94th Infantry moved into Germany, the wall was still partially there. The Russians had built it to keep their people from moving out. Many lost their lives trying to get to freedom from Russia.

It was winter when we entered Germany, but I was accustomed to the cold. We were a powerful force, able to overcome the enemy. One of the box cars on a train we took over was full of beautiful, expensive linens. I took some and sent them home. We did a lot of damage to buildings, especially businesses. Sometimes we slept in the fields, covering ourselves with hay. A cow almost stepped on me once.

As we moved along, we took a lot of prisoners. They seemed to be happy to surrender. Those captured were trucked back to the base and sent on to prisoner-of-war camps. We treated them like humans, and they responded to our good treatment. They seemed happy to be caught. I befriended two citizens and was invited into their home.

I saw the railroad cars that were used to take people to the concentration camps. Nazi youth were seen around in their uniforms.

There were weeks at a time when we didn't have facilities for showering and didn't change clothes nor shave. We must have been quite a sight.

You don't get mail when you're on the battlefield. Sometimes my letters were months old before I got them. I was not paid regularly. There was no place to spend it anyway. My pay was $21.00 a month.

Driving truck became my first job upon leaving the military. I was able to make more money when I switched to driving semis. I hauled all kinds of auto parts.

After being home a couple years in Sault St. Marie, I married a woman who at eighteen hired into Dow Chemical as a manager. We had three children. Our oldest boy was in the Vietnam War. The youngest became a minister. Our daughter lives in Attica.

For twenty-five years I cared for a rich, retired lawyer, doing everything you can imagine for him. He changed shirts two or three times on hot days because he didn't want to have on sweaty shirts. His laundry bill was very big. I met important people in this job, Ilitch, the owner of the Tigers being one.

We lived in Warren at this time. The lawyer lived in Bloomfield Hills. I worked until I was 95 years old.

16

Calvin Winters ~ I Wanted In The Army

People call me Cal, but Calvin Winters is my name. I was born in Maryland in 1927. I have one sister and one half-sister. My dad worked for the Baltimore Railroad. I worked there also. My job was replacing the loose bricks in the ceiling of the tunnels that had worked loose due to the vibration of the traffic above.

I enlisted in the Army. If I had waited to be drafted, I would have had no choice – and I wanted Army! Also, I would have had to sign up for four years. I had to sign up only for three years by enlisting. I went to boot camp in Camp Polk in Louisiana. There we did hikes and mainly spent time with our rifles. We learned to assemble, clean, and shoot (accurately) our rifles.

From there, I was sent to Fort Dix Motor Pool. My next destination was to be sent to the island of Honshu in Japan. A very short time before we were to ship out, the atomic bomb was dropped on Japan, and the war was soon over. My trip to Honshu was cancelled. For the rest of my time, I stayed at Fort Dix driving trucks and sometimes busses when groups of men had to be transported. Our trucks hauled all sorts of supplies for the camp from food to equipment. As the need for fewer men grew, I was discharged after serving two and a half years of the three years I signed up for.

I was glad to see the war end and lucky I didn't have to leave the states. I had two uncles and three cousins who were not lucky. None of them survived the war.

I signed up for the reserves. I missed the Korean War by three years.

Before enlisting, I had a girlfriend. I decided to not have contact while I was in the service. I didn't want her to possibly experience my not coming home. After the war we were married and eventually had thirteen children – nine girls and four boys.

Jobs were scarce right after the war. Some businesses that were purely war-related, like making parachutes, were closed for good. Others closed temporarily for changing over to non-military production, like the vehicle industries.

At this time, my wife and our twin daughters went to Michigan to visit relatives. Within a week I had a job at Ford Motor Company where I worked until retirement.

We have stayed in Michigan since. My wife has passed away but my children – all thirteen of them – established homes within fifteen miles from me. Thirty-seven grandchildren and over one hundred great grandchildren make my life complete.

17

Donald Steiner ~ Two Kamikazi Planes Came: We Got Them

I, Donald Steiner, was born in 1925 in Clarkston, Michigan. I had one sister and two brothers. The older brother was in the Navy; so was my dad. My dad was on the USS Constellation during World War I.

During my last year of high school, at seventeen, I enlisted in the Navy. I went immediately to Great Lakes, Chicago, Illinois, for training. I was first assigned to the Naval Armed Guard as part of a gun crew. In New Orleans, Louisiana, I boarded my first ship, the SS Alpha, an oil tanker. For the next three months we hauled crude oil to various ports along the eastern seaboard. This was a dangerous mission for German submarines were known to cruise that area. We frequently made contact with these subs while sailing in these seas and into the Caribbean Sea on the SS Alpha and SS Cornelia.

The port at San Juan, Puerto Rico, was closed from sunset until dawn with a heavy metal net to keep out submarines. We arrived during the closed hours. I was on watch then and noticed something beyond the net I could not identify. I called the ship's captain and my naval officer to the bridge. They could not identify it either. The net was opened so we could enter, and a destroyer was sent out. The next morning, we received word that the destroyer had engaged a submarine and had sunk it.

Following this, I was aboard a Liberty Ship (freighter), the SS Benjamin Goodhue, bound for naval operations in North Africa, Sicily, and Italy. This trip across the Atlantic took us seventeen days. We were part of a convoy travelling about fourteen miles per hour.

Of course, in the Mediterranean Sea we encountered more German submarine attacks. At the same time, we were dealing with frequent air raid sirens warning us of the German "STUKA" dive bombers' expected arrival in Naples, Italy.

After about eight months of this, I returned to the United States where I was assigned to the Naval Amphibious Forces in Fort Pierce, Florida, and Norfolk, Virginia, for training. When trained, I was assigned to an LST-15 (Landing Ship Tank – the Navy's largest amphibious ship).

We sailed through the Panama Canal to the South Pacific into Pearl Harbor. Here I was promoted to Boatswain's Mate 2/C and transferred to the LST-45.

One month later, I found myself, along with General MacArthur's troops, involved in the invasion of the Philippine Islands. General MacArthur was fulfilling his promise, "I will return." Little did I know he expected me to tag along.

A few days later, we invaded Leyte, firing from our ship. We were back and forth among the other nearby islands of Guam, Saipan, and Ie Shima (Ie Shima is part of Okinawa). Ie Shima is where the famous war correspondent, Ernie Pyle, was killed and buried.

We took troops back and forth between the Philippines and the islands. We were at Leyte with other ships including two liberty freighters when two Kamikaze planes came over. Within two minutes our anti-aircraft guns set the first one on fire. As it headed for our ship it veered off and crashed into the liberty ship near us, setting the ship on fire.

Within two minutes the second plane crossed our ship's stern as we continued firing at it, and it crashed into the second liberty ship as she was unloading 650 tons of gasoline and ammunition. The liberty continued exploding and setting the ship on fire. All hands abandoned the ship as she sank.

Five days earlier, near Mindanao, the Marcus Daly was struck by a kamikaze plane which made a hole in the bow large enough to drive a train through!

Later, we were again in battle on the Japanese island of Okinawa and Ie Shema.

During this time, two significant things happened: President Roosevelt died, and Harry S. Truman became president. Then VE Day happened.

The island of Ulithi was where Pacific forces met for rest and relaxation. Since we damaged our ship on the coral reef, we left the Caroline Islands and returned to Guam for repairs via Saipan and Tinian in the Mariana Islands.

It was here in Tinian that I celebrated my twentieth birthday and my Christian birthday. At the Navy Seabee Chapel, I felt the call and accepted Jesus Christ as my Savior.

Repairs could not be made in Hawaii nor Guam, so we were ordered back to San Diego, California. Midway to San Diego, the Japanese surrendered. VJ Day was August 14, 1945. The Armistice was signed on the USS Missouri in Tokyo Bay.

After the end, we were all anxious to go home. I was three points short of being near the front of the line. They said I had to go to sea again on a destroyer. I said, "NO!", but they sent me home on leave before I was to be shipped out. When I returned home, Marge and I were married.

An error in my favor was made in my points, and I was allowed to go home to be discharged. In my three-and-one-half years of service, I had been at sea thirty-one months on five different ships. I travelled aboard ships far enough to have gone around the world.

Marge and I had four daughters and a son. I went to college at Pontiac Business Institute and Detroit Bible College. I got my Clarkston High School diploma through a new system for World War II veterans who were honorably discharged. School officials invited Marge and me out to lunch to celebrate, and I joined the 475 current graduating seniors, leading them in receiving diplomas at Pine Knob.

I worked at various corporations in the accounting field, later hiring in at G.M. Truck and Bus Group in the accounting department.

I retired from there after twenty-four years. We now reside in Oxford, Michigan.

I am well aware, however, that all of this recognition was because I represented all of those who served their country during World War II, and I humbly accepted it as such. God has been good to me.

18

Bill Cheolas ~ The Gliders Came In First

I was born, Bill Cheolas, in Detroit in 1924. There were five of us kids, two brothers younger than I and two sisters. One brother served in the Korean War.

In 1942, at the age of 18, I enlisted in the Army Air Corps. That was not my intention to do so at all. In high school, I decided that in order

64 | HELEN O. BIGELOW

to get a good job, I had to get some skills. I really didn't know what skills to look for, but I learned the Navy was advertising for people to join the Navy and learn skills for the future.

Two friends and I often rode our bikes down the street to the airfield to watch the planes come and go. About then, the Army Air Corps advertised that the Army Air Corps needed pilots. For that program, you had to pass an exam. I thought, "Why not". I was only a C student and really had my doubts I could pass the exam but decided to take it. My dad had to sign papers for me to take the exam. Surprise, surprise, I passed!

I got on a train with many other men and five days later found myself in Miami Beach, Florida. Our boot camp there lasted ten to fifteen weeks. Then, we were sent to San Antonio, Texas, to learn rules and regulations for pilots. In Cuero, Texas, we had seventy hours of primary training in small planes with open cockpits. We continued on into basic training from where we were working with larger, more powerful, and faster planes. We worked with planes from the lighter, sleek fighter planes to the larger bombers. If at any point a student failed to pass required knowledge, he was transferred to a different course in the Air Corps like radio technician or navigator.

At this point, we were to decide if we preferred to work with fighter planes or heavy bombers. Then in McAllan, Texas, we practiced what we had learned while waiting for our next orders.

I worked a lot with gliders. Gliders had two pilots and were pulled with heavy one-inch ropes by C47's. On the front was a loop of rope so a plane could swoop down and hook onto the rope to retrieve the glider. The glider had two smaller ski-like slides on the front that dug into the ground and acted like brakes. A glider, when empty of machinery, can carry fifteen men plus the two pilots. When men are jumping out, all fifteen are dropped within a half mile.

Our unit was involved in seven invasions, six in Europe and one in Borneo. On one invasion, the British Army had gone ahead and put a smoke screen along the Rhine River for us. A lot had dissipated by the time we got there. Our glider had a Jeep with four men when they landed twelve miles into German territory. They were bringing in reinforcements allowing the allies to attack the Germans from two directions. The German soldiers were on one side of the Rhine and the allies on the other. Our men were part of the 17th Airborne Division, helping ground troops.

The glider landing was a difficult one because there were electric transmission lines right where we needed to land. A decision was made to line up the glider and go underneath the lines. It was a hairy decision, but it worked.

These were very dangerous missions, but one pilot went on five of them. He was to land offshore in Italy. Offshore, the Navy was giving firing support for a safe glider landing. However, somehow messages were confused resulting in the glider being shot down by the Navy. Since water was only four feet deep there, the pilot and men survived with only shrapnel wounds.

In some South Pacific landings, mules were hauled in instead of Jeeps because gas would not be available for Jeeps.

Post war, I hauled two hundred five-gallon containers of gas at a time in a C47.

In the South Pacific's many islands there was a need for up-to-date maps. I flew a four-engine B17 while photographers took pictures of the Philippine Islands and many others. We flew out of the Philippines and Borneo.

While in Borneo, we stayed in the summer home of Sir Roger Brook. This man gained notoriety when he settled disputes among the tribes of Borneo. The tribes had been fighting for years, and he convinced them how life would be so much better if they stopped fighting.

After the war, I flew to the airfield where incoming planes were bringing in wounded people. I flew them to hospitals.

In Fort Benning, Georgia, I taught glider pilots. In Oklahoma, I instructed men to fly B25's. I was discharged in Oklahoma and returned to Detroit. I didn't know what I wanted to do. I thought about commercial passenger pilot, but that was in its infancy. There wasn't much flying in winter because there were no reliable instruments for flying in bad weather.

Selfridge Field contacted me. They needed reserves. But I'd had enough of the military and refused.

My brother was in the poultry business and needed help with hatching baby chicks. I helped him. I took a poultry class at Michigan State University. Later, I worked for a big poultry company for four years. Then I went into business for myself.

At this time, some nurses at the hospital were eating at the restaurant where I ate twice a week. One of them later became my wife.

One day the local high school principal called me to substitute in science and vocational agricultural classes. I went back to college and got my degree. I taught for many years, finally retiring in 1988. My wife decided it was time for her to retire also. My wife is no longer with me, but our son lives with me in Melvin, Michigan.

19

Charles Carson ~ Sandblasting With Ground Walnut Shells

I, Charles Carson, was born in Ecorse, Michigan, in 1925. I had a mixture of siblings and half sisters and brothers. Since this was in the Depression Era, it was difficult making a living with a large family. I quit school at 17 to help support the family. Grandpa helped a lot by growing a big garden including the food that would keep a long time like potatoes, squash, carrots, and beets.

My dad was a finish carpenter, and work was scarce at times unless it was a circular staircase job. No one else around seemed to know how to build those.

When I was 18, I enlisted in the Navy. I would rather have a roof over my head and three meals a day than sleep in the open, walk through mud with a heavy pack on my back, and carry a heavy rifle. I went to boot camp in Farragut, Idaho. We had boat drills and swimming lessons. We were taught to dive feet-first with our arms crossed at our chest. This was to keep the water from going up our nose. We were taught how to properly salute, who to salute, and how to use and care for our rifle. After boot camp, we were allowed to go on leave. We went on an old train with a steam engine that puffed out a lot of smoke.

My next stop was Norman, Oklahoma. My first choice for an occupation was to go to radio school. However, I was in the hospital with something they called "Cat Fever", whatever that was, and missed the boat. My second choice was aircraft mechanics' school. In six months, I graduated.

In Quonset, Rhode Island, we were to clean aircraft parts. These were all metal and had to be sandblasted. However, we didn't use sand. We used ground-up walnut shells. They came out of that hose with such force that they did the job just fine. The hose got away from one of the guys, was swinging wildly, and tore his pants off. He was in pain for some time.

We shipped out from San Francisco, heading for the South Pacific. The trip was noisy for the gunnery unit did their practicing then.

If we crossed the equator and international dateline, there were initiations for those who had not done it before. They paddled us as we ran through a long tent, shaved my head, and did everything to us they could think of. We earned certificates depending on how many times we had crossed those points. You don't want a shaved head in the tropics.

Our destination was the combat zone. We arrived at Espiritu Santo. One day my buddy and I decided to go dove hunting. We heard snapping of twigs as we entered the jungle. We walked, rested, walked, and heard twigs snapping that weren't ours. We saw small pigs – several of them. Then we heard the noise getting closer and closer while checking our guns in case it was Japs. Suddenly a big, about 400-pound pig came out of the jungle. It was the mother of those little pigs! We took off.

This was in the New Hebrides Islands, northeast of Australia. This was job "aviators overhaul". We worked on engines, planes, replaced parts, reassembled, and tested for six or seven months.

Then, we were on the Orate Peninsula of Guadalcanal. We were just a reserve unit in transit to Henderson Field. This was a nice place with a lot of coconut palms and foliage plants. There was less work, so we had free time.

The Red Cross set up near the airstrip to have coffee and donuts available. The problem was they SOLD donuts and coffee to Americans, but they were FREE to Brits and other military personnel.

There were a lot of big battles before the Americans took Guadalcanal. The war was over when we were in Guam again, but there was still a lot of fighting going on. Four Marines were killed. Big crates of engines sat on the dock ready to be taken out and dumped in the sea. As the crates were moved, large roaches scurried out. The locals grabbed those 1 ½" x 4" insects, broke them in two, and ate them like candy.

Both in the Philippines and Guam, snipers were a big problem. The jungle was so thick, the enemy could step out, fire, and step back before we could even see them.

We listened to Tokyo Rose because she had on good American music. We didn't pay much attention to her talks.

There were still a lot of Japs on the islands. If you could hear them shooting, it meant you were still alive. There were two times when I was really scared: 1. I was in Guam heading back to my hut when I saw a water bag nearby. I bent to pick it up, made a hole in it and took a swallow. When I stood up, a bullet hit where my head had been.

2. After I had spent four days patching holes on the wing of a plane, a sniper took a poke at me. The sniper missed me as I slid off the wing, but he put two more holes in the plane that I had just completed the job on! Then I was frustrated because I didn't know if I was mad because I'd been shot at or because I now had two more holes to fix.

Before heading home, we were on Cebu Island. It was a fierce battle. Eight hundred men went into battle. One hundred twenty came out.

There were a lot of bananas on these islands. When bananas are ripened on the plant, they are pink – and so delicious!

All the equipment on the islands had to be taken apart, loaded on boats, and taken out to sea, even the planes. Souvenirs could be taken if it was Japanese. American things were considered government issue.

When we got the news that the bombs had been dropped on Japan, we knew we'd soon be going home. When I first got home, I just laid around. Then I used the G.I. bill to go to aviation mechanics' school and earned my Federal Aviation License. I had to go to school even though I'd had a lot of experience because military and civilian planes are quite different.

Although we had written all during the war, when I came home, I saw my future wife for the first time. We were married a few weeks later. We had two boys.

I worked at a couple jobs before going into Continental Motors where I was the most experienced mechanic repairing parts and making experimental parts. I worked there until retirement.

No matter where you've been or who you are, you've had good times and bad times if you've been in the military. The times I've had trouble since I came home were when a guy got his jollies by seeing me jump. He would come up behind me and make a loud, sharp noise that made me jump.

I've had a lot of good years here in Muskegon, Michigan, with my son and his wife next door. My wife is in rehab right now, but I expect she'll be home soon.

20

Heinz Anger ~ Fighting In Hitler's Army

I, Heinz Anger, was born in Rostock, Germany, in 1921. I had one sister. My father fought in World War I and mom was a homemaker. My father was a trained butcher. We owned our own successful meat/butchery business until the Russians occupied the territory and destroyed everything we had.

When I was eleven, I was encouraged to join the Hitler Youth Program, but my parents were not interested, and I was able to say, "No". Adolph Hitler established a program where parents had to register

74 | HELEN O. BIGELOW

their sons with the German government at ten years old, and military training was provided when you turned eighteen. If you didn't register the son, the parents were taken to court. It was mandatory.

We had no choice but to be drafted, and I entered at the age of 17. (If you didn't go, you were never seen again.)

After completing my parachute training, I was assigned to the First Parachute Division. We could not choose what division. Fallschirmjäger was my assignment in southern Italy. My training for this was grueling and intensive for six months.

The most memorable experience I had during my time in the war was being in the Battle of Monte Cassino in Italy. It was one of the bloodiest battles close to the hearts of many Italians. This battle was very personal to me because my commanding officer was killed. He gave me orders to go to a certain area on a hill with my weapon. I knew this was not a good spot because there was no cover. I told him, "No". I wanted to be higher up behind rocks. Normally I would not have argued with my superior, but I just had a feeling. My commander was in that position for five minutes and was killed before my eyes. All I could think about was that it could have been me. I fought in battles around Monte Cassino against Polish, South African, New Zealand, British, and American forces.

One thing you don't realize is planes have to fly higher in the mountains. As a paratrooper, the longer you're in the air, the longer you're a target.

The bombing of Cassino lasted twelve hours – constantly bombing. We were supposed to have mortar protection. Well once we were out of ammunition, that was it.

As Germany's withdrawal continued in northern Italy, our unit formed a defense along the Po River. I had a machine gun protecting us as we crossed the bridge which was to be destroyed after we crossed. They made a mistake and blew it up before we got across.

Soon after, I was caught by the Polish and turned over to the British 8th Army, shipped over to Bari, Italy, and then sent to Egypt where the British POW camp was. Just think, I had shot some of their people, but they were fair. They actually had me working in an office translating for them because I could read, write, and speak some English. We received 1/3 loaf of bread with some tomato paste each day. Since in combat, we had very little food, if any. I was content with the small amount. At home, bread, soup, pig ears, and pig tails were often all we could find to eat, and we were happy to have that.

We were not able to communicate with our family during the combat years, and it was a year before my family received a letter telling them that I was in a POW camp in Africa. I was there for two-and-a-half years.

At war's end, it took me three years to get home. The British helped me. I was sent to East Germany. There I worked at my parents' meat-packing plant.

I got married and had two children. We escaped to West Germany one night and lived there one year before coming to Michigan. My wife's aunt sponsored us so we could come. I applied for a government meat inspector job and retired from there thirty years later.

I now live in Macomb County, living the American Dream.

HELEN O. BIGELOW

21

Emerson Kennedy ~ Dodging Submarines In The Pacific

My name is Emerson Kennedy. I was born here in this house near Cass City, Michigan, 96 years ago. My family were farmers. My dad bought this farm and bought this house from Sears Roebuck for $1,263.

It was pre-cut, each piece marked and boxed, ready to be assembled. I had one brother and one sister.

When I was eighteen, I was drafted into the Army and sent for basic training in Camp Fannin, Texas. In Fort Sheridan I had been issued my clothes and everything to put in my duffle bag. These were passed to me by German POWs. They were in other camps working at jobs like cutting hair and picking up garbage for the trucks.

We were preparing to go to Europe, but that part of the war was now over. Instead, we were sent to San Francisco to board ships for the South Pacific. The voyage was something else! We zig-zagged across the Pacific dodging areas where they thought there might be submarines.

We stopped in Hawaii to pick up supplies and then continued on to the Philippine Islands. There were too many ships in our convoy to go on to Japan. We were to be replacements for an invasion that didn't happen.

Our troop carrier anchored, and we took landing crafts ashore at Manila in the Philippines. North of Manila, we joined another replacement unit at Linguyan Gulf Base which was part of the 6th Infantry Anti-Tank Division. We stayed here six weeks or so, living in tents, and firing the anti-tank destroyer ammunition.

We left the 120-degree weather of the islands and arrived in Korea to cold, snowy weather. We survived a typhoon on our way to Korea. In Inchon, Korea, in the middle of Halloween night, the troops were unloaded followed by the Jeeps, trucks, and other equipment and supplies. That's when I discovered my duffle bag was missing. All I had were the clothes on my back. For the next month, friends my size loaned me clothes until the supply sergeant could get me some through the military.

From there our company took a train to Andong. There we were to guard a large building. We put up tents, established a guard schedule and settled in. We wondered what was in that building that was so valuable to have twenty-four-hour guards for a month. Some told us it was full of rice. After some time, an officer decided it was time to find out what was in the building. Locks were broken and the doors opened. It was an empty building!

Our battalion was moved to Kague. There my rank changed to corporal and then to Buck Sergeant. We were to guard the town, the base, and all equipment. I pulled guard duty a month at a time. Wherever we went the bases had pretty well been vacated and we replacements were in full control. After being in combat for months, everyone was anxious to get home.

One person that was around was a boy about twelve years old who seemed to make himself a friend to all of us. He was scarred from having survived the atomic bombing of his homeland. Being of a mischievous nature, he was always into things and getting into trouble. The soldiers were always coming to his rescue.

A sergeant of the night guard came in. I had had my breakfast and went to my tent to sleep. I was rudely awakened by being kicked and punched. I was told not to get mad (which I was) because I had fifteen minutes to pack since I was going home. A Jeep was waiting to take me to the train.

I was discharged in Illinois. Several of us heading in the same direction hired a cab to take us to the train. It was great to be back with my family and my girlfriend. She and I reconnected and were married several months later. We raised two girls and a boy.

My father wanted off the farm, so he got a job in Marlette and I bought the farm. I worked at Saginaw Steel for four years, but I found it to be extremely cold work in winter. I worked the farm, working in timber also when I had time.

My last job was driving a school bus. I thought eight years of that hassle was enough. About 1985, my wife and I decided to go to Germany and look up some of my family. We learned some interesting facts about members of my family.

My second cousin was drafted into the German Army at twelve years of age. During basic training, he won a medal for marksmanship. Later he was sent to the Russian front. He wasn't happy about that, so he slipped away across a nearby river – into the hands of the Americans who arrested him.

I also learned that my mother's two military sons were leased to Great Britain and sent to Archangel, Russia, to help keep strategic rivers open so supplies could get through.

I have, since my wife and handicapped son passed away, lived here on the farm alone. One of my daughters lives nearby. I keep active in caring for myself with a little help from my daughter.

22

Edward Swartz ~ Three Of My Ships Sank

I am Edward Swartz. I was born in Hazel Park, Michigan, in 1924. I had two sisters and three brothers. Brother John entered the Navy at 17 and retired thirty years later. Brother Joe went into the Army. My third brother, Mike, was not eligible to serve, but years later went to college and became a warrant officer.

My father and his brothers were carpenters. Before college, my brother did the lathe work for them.

I enlisted in the Navy and was first sent to Great Lakes for basic training. From there I was sent to California for more training before I was sent to the South Pacific. I was on the destroyer, USS Benham, headed for Hawaii. We headed south to the Solomon Islands and ran into quite a nest of islands occupied by the Japanese. Our first big challenge was Guadalcanal. Driving the Japanese out of there was not a one-day battle. (At this point, I had been in the Navy for one year.)

Nearby was another hot spot, Palagi. We lost the battle here and the Benham was sunk. Those of us who survived were picked up by the Lang who happened to be nearby. The Benham was cut in half by a submarine. Some men lost their lives in the ship's destruction while others drowned. We survivors were taken aboard to be part of the crew on the Helena. Unfortunately, that ship was sunk also, but I was in the hospital with an infection at the time. Big freighters were being converted to small carriers which were more in demand. If these carriers or other ships were attacked and were close to us, we rescued pilots and crews. Our destroyers were not deep, so we could easily pull people up our ladders into our ships.

When we were near Australia our ships were taken to port to have the barnacles scraped off the bottom and the bottoms repainted. This was important for the barnacles caused drag and slowed the ships down. They had to be jacked up for this procedure.

One of our carriers was bombed. Planes returning could not land on the ship. Pilots flying high enough could parachute out to be picked up. Those who went down into the water in their planes escaped as best they could into the oil-slicked surface. Some were badly injured. Some were so covered with oil they couldn't see. As we pulled those up onto our ship, they were taken to New Caledonia Island. We estimated we had saved 300 men. We received awards for the operation we did. We stayed in New Caledonia for some time, living in tents and roughing it.

Our crew was credited with sinking eleven submarines. The Benham was blown up by a torpedo but was able to navigate. Each compartment on these ships was air-tight and sealed with thick, metal doors to keep them afloat.

When we were sent back to the states, we were on guard duty – COPS. These sailors had been away three years and when they got home, sometimes they got in trouble. My job was to keep them in line.

When I arrived home, I did more than my share of drinking and fighting. I was always ready to do both. Finally, my dad told me to stop it or get out. I stopped.

My dad built homes. He hired me to work with him. He gave each of us a lot to build our homes on.

I married a beautiful woman, and we raised four boys and a girl.

My wife and daughter are both gone. I live alone here in my home in Lapeer, Michigan.

23

Burney James (Jim) Elliott ~ We Get Even With The Army

My name is Burney James (Jim) Elliott. I was born in Marlette, one of nine children. My father was a decorator, painting and papering houses. He died when I was three, leaving mom alone with all of us kids. It was a hard life back then with no help.

At this time, we could sign up at seventeen for enlistment if a parent signed for us. We were not to be called for duty though until we were eighteen. Mom signed for me. I was called at eighteen when I was part way through the twelfth grade. I didn't get to attend my graduation. I was in the Navy!

I had six weeks of boot camp at Great Lakes in Illinois. We learned to defend ourselves and accurately shoot a gun. The war ended while I was in boot camp. I boarded the SS Wisconsin and headed for the South Pacific by sailing through the Panama Canal. I was on this battleship my whole time in the military. Going back home, my job was damage control. Of course, since the war was over, there was no damage. We had gone only as far as San Diego when we turned around and went through the Panama Canal again. We stopped in Cuba and picked up three hundred Army men who were expecting to be discharged when they reached home. They were really cocky, thinking they were superior to us, and treated us like servants. We missed their connecting boat, so they missed their date to be discharged. Our ship took them to Norfolk, Virginia. I stayed on ship returning to the Cuba area in the Atlantic. There were only four ports big enough for our ship – San Diego, Seattle, Norfolk, and New York. I was on that ship for thirteen months.

When we signed up, we had to sign up for the duration of the war plus six months. When my six months was up, I went home and was discharged. I went back to twelfth grade and graduated with the class that was behind me.

With all the military returning and factories cutting back, jobs were scarce, at least in the Marlette area. I took a job shoveling coal on a ship by hand – one time!!

I was married and we had five boys and a girl.

In 1951, I joined the Reserves. I was sent to Biggs Army Air Force base in El Paso, Texas. I was trained as an automotive mechanic, working exclusively on cars.

Selfridge Field called me back where I stayed for three years.

Returning home, I worked at a second job for thirty years at Marlette Oil and Gas. My main jobs were eighteen years at a trailer factory and eleven years at a men's clothing store. I always was able to keep working.

24

Anonymous ~ Dual Citizenship Becomes A Problem

I was born in Florida in 1925, but my parents were Canadian. We had dual citizenship moving back and forth between Windsor and

Florida. This became a real problem when I started school. I started school in Florida when I was six years old but moved to Windsor when I was seven years old. Of course, Canadians were on the metric system while here we have the decimal system. They studied different people and events in history. In the confusion, in Florida we had no kindergarten. My sister in Florida was ahead of me one year but when my mother gave up trying to deal with the dual school situation, my sister came home each day and taught me what she had learned that day. I wound up skipping a couple grades.

When in Windsor, my Florida accent got me in a lot of trouble. As others teased me, my red hair and temper got me in a lot of fights.

Since I had dual citizenship, I wound up having to register for the draft in three places. An American friend and I bought a camper and moved to Pasadena, California. We registered there too. My friend had deferment papers, but I enlisted in the Navy – in the Seabees. I didn't want to go into the Army, so I enlisted so I could choose. Seabees are construction people. I was around that for my dad repaired the cars of northerners while he was in Florida until the Depression came along.

Boot camp in Virginia was in undeveloped land. We had to clear the land and put up all the necessary buildings a base would require: toilets, cafeterias, medical building, and sleeping quarters.

From there, we went to an old camp along the Gulf Coast, marching distance from the Mississippi River. This was a large shipping area.

Our next destination was the South Pacific via the Panama Canal. We built Henderson Field with the Japanese watching on one side and us working on the other side. We went from place to place, building bases and roads for the vehicles. This was jungle territory, so we had a lot of clearing to do.

In the area northeast of Australia are many islands, many with just natives who spoke no known language. The Japanese occupied many of these islands under a mandate system. It's like renting a house. They occupied it and took care of it until someone came and took possession and ownership of it.

OUR HEROES NEXT DOOR | 89

Guadalcanal was occupied by the Japanese under the mandate system. It took a lot of fierce fighting for the Americans to take possession. Japan was in the process of building an airfield there.

Japan had control of the Solomon Islands until we arrived. There are many mountainous islands there with a lot of Japanese on them. It took a lot of heavy battles to get the Japanese out of the mountains. Since the Japanese didn't own the islands, they didn't want to fight for them, so they headed north to be closer to their homeland. Many didn't make it.

We returned to the Philippines to a camp south of Manilla. It has a protected shipping bay with a large cave for storage. The outside consists of farming terraces. This was a holding port for us. Many of the Japanese had headed towards home before we arrived.

We had a firm hold on the south islands. In Manilla, we roamed around if we wanted to. I could requisition a Jeep to look around. The stores were full of beautiful dishes that would make nice souvenirs, but I didn't think I could get them home without breaking them. I found a Japanese rifle (military) in great shape I really wanted. But, again, getting it home would be a problem. People stealing others' souvenirs was a problem too.

In the Philippine Islands, there was fighting all around us, but we were not involved in it. I wanted to see the Walled City before I left, but I didn't get to do it.

People were desperate for meat. They were cutting down trees, leaving an 18-inch block for chopping up horses. The business section of town was all shot up. The women came out of their stores, lifted their skirts, and peed on the street-side. You saw no men around. They had all gone to war. We were here in the Philippines for a year.

We had a military base in Emirau which is a volcanic island, round in shape but open in the center with one opening big enough for ships to go in and out. Here ships could safely transfer supplies from one to the other. Emirau was a German mandate. The Japanese were in control in northern areas, and we were in control in most of the southern

Pacific area. We had PT boats protecting ships of ours passing through the southern area.

Just before shipping out for home, I went to the submarine base where as far as I could see both ways were submarines hooked up to tenders. Tenders were supply providers for the submarines.

When returning to San Francisco, so many ships were returning home that all ports were busy, and they had difficulty finding a place for us. At home I studied radar and solar. I then found work repairing radios. I worked for Philco TV building and repairing sets, working my way up to supervisor.

I married the sister of my two best friends who did not return from the war. She also had dual citizenship. We made our home in Windsor. We adopted one son. I now live in Lapeer, Michigan, at Stonegate, a retirement facility.

AUTHOR'S NOTE: This guy looking at all the souvenirs said he found a Japanese rifle but didn't know if he could get it home. He was a very, very soft-spoken fellow – almost whispering. I have difficulty hearing. I thought he said he found a Japanese WIFE. I asked him if he got married. He said, "Married! No!". I said, "Didn't you say you found a Japanese wife?" He laughed and said, "No! I said RIFLE". We all had a good laugh.

25

Andrew Duke ~ Guarding At The Hospital

I, Andrew "Andy" Duke, was born in Detroit. During the war, at the age of 17, I enlisted with the Navy. I enlisted for "the duration of the war" so when the war was over, I would be sent home.

After enlisting, I was sent to Great Lakes for basic training. From there, I went to a Navy hospital in Texas. There, I was trained to be a nurse and did whatever the nurses told me to do.

I was sent to Okinawa attached to a Navy Field Hospital as a Pharmacist Mate. I didn't have to work in the hospital. My job was to stand guard duty around the hospital several hundred yards away. I did hear about a Pharmacist Mate who had to do appendicitis surgery while on a submarine. There were no doctors on the subs.

The hospital I guarded treated mostly wounded Marines and some Navy men from Kamikaze attacks. In 1945 the atomic bomb was dropped, but we still had wounded men coming in. The Japs were still fighting.

In January of 1946, I was sent back from Okinawa through Seattle on an aircraft carrier. Immediately after I got off, supplies were grabbed, and the ship went for another load. They were bringing back 10,000 to 12,000 men at a time.

I'm thankful that I never had to shoot anyone, and no one shot at me. I enjoyed my time in the Navy. They treated me good. My older brother was in the Marine Corps for four years in World War II. My younger brother served in the Korean War and in the Vietnam War. He was a career soldier. I have one surviving sister.

When I came back, I returned to Detroit. In 1947 I went to work for the New York Central Railroad. It was a good job, and many of the guys returning went to work there. It was there that I met my wife, and we were married. We had four children.

I worked at the railroad for forty-two years and retired in 1988. I was a brakeman sometimes, and sometimes I was the conductor. My last job was running from 17 Mile Road in Sterling Heights to Elkhart, Indiana. We moved to Allenton where I still live.

26

Arthur Morton Fishman ~ Military Acknowledges My Jewish Heritage

My name is Arthur Morton Fishman. I was born in Highland Park, Michigan, in 1927. Dad was a professional painter. I had one sister.

My friends and I – about 14 of us – saw that a test was to be given for qualifying for enlisting in the Army Air Corps. We were doubtful we could pass the test but took it anyway. We passed the test and were enlisted in the Army Air Corps. However, six weeks later we were discharged. So many were interested in the program they had to cancel it.

After taking another test, we enlisted again – in the Navy! I was credited with two years of service for the six weeks I was in the Army Air Corps.

I met two others who became very close friends for many years, one from Lake Orion where I had lived.

I was trained as a diesel engineer. I replaced the engineer who worked under deck keeping things in our ship operating smoothly. That was my post most of my entire military career.

We were in Okinawa at holiday time. We were told to put on our dress uniforms for we were going to Shanghai for Jewish temple services – Rosh ha sha nah. I said I wasn't going, but I changed my mind. I missed the bus, so I didn't go. Ten days later there was another holiday. A rickshaw took me to the Russian quarter where the service was to be held. I was told to not pay the rickshaw driver more than 15 cents for the three-mile trip. All I had was two dimes, so he received a bonus.

I hesitated to go to the temple services for I had never attended any when growing up. I didn't know any of the Jewish protocol like praying standing up. Praying kneeling was considered worshiping a man – Jesus.

While I was below deck, I used spare time to study. In the time of seven months, I had studied enough to raise my rank three steps.

Our destroyers were escorts for other ships, mainly carriers. Carriers needed protection because they were pretty vulnerable. The bodies were made with a steel frame, but the rest of the ship was wood. Men on those ships were called TIN CAN SAILORS.

When I took a turn as a pointer, no one told me to belt myself to the ship. A pointer watches when big shells were fired to see if they were accurate in hitting their targets. As my first shell was fired, the pressure knocked me to the deck. I learned quickly why belts were worn.

Our ship, the U.S.S. Robinson, left Okinawa with a load of mail headed for Shanghai, China. There the mail was distributed to other ships heading in many directions

Sometimes the destroyers were used for various duties like as mine sweepers to clear waters near the islands so ships could get closer to land. Escorting carriers was our main job. It took destroyers thirteen hours to get a carrier through the Panama Canal. There were destroyers leading the carrier and destroyers following the carrier through the canal. They had started in Pearl Harbor.

At the time of the Armistice, four destroyers left Shanghai, China, and headed for the Philippines. I was below deck and as we grew closer to the Philippines the noise level grew. As it increased it was just a loud noise and I was afraid I was missing some important message. Were we being attacked? Should I send a message of some kind? My chief came up and saw I was concerned. He told me to take off my ear protectors. The noise was loud laughing and shouting. The people on shore were celebrating the end of the war! From on deck the American flag could be seen flying over the Philippine Islands!

General MacArthur was well known for his many battles in the Philippine Islands. Many of the locals joined him in driving the Japanese out.

When General MacArthur was fired, there were mixed emotions. The military praised him for all the success he had in defeating the Japanese in the area. The government thought he was taking over and doing things his way.

In returning to the United States and we sailors were given leave, sometimes things got a little wild. I was given shore patrol – with a gun. I told my superior I was not qualified to carry a gun. Chief said it was okay, there weren't any bullets in it.

After leaving the military, I concentrated on getting an education, preparing me for the successful life in several businesses. One challenge was working in the Housing and Urban Development (HUD) corporation.

Since my second retirement I'm keeping very busy with being involved with several Jewish service organizations. I'm spending my days enjoying the work and the many interesting people I met of all faiths and nationalities. Through my 95 years I've been to many places and am thankful to be able to continue.

Art with his good friend Lt. Col. Jefferson, a survivor of the Tuskegee Squadron of Alabama.

AUTHOR'S NOTE: For a man of his age, Arthur lives an exhausting life. His days are filled with tasks in leadership positions demanding skill and energy of one much younger than he. He is a real blessing to those who know him.

27

Cornelia Fort ~ The Arizona Went Down

Cornelia Fort was born into a family of privilege near Nashville, Tennessee. Rejecting the debutant scene and acting more like a "tomboy", Cornelia's lifestyle led her in a different direction than her family expected.

In her youth, she overheard her father lecture her three brothers about how dangerous airplanes were and he didn't want to hear of them being in one. Cornelia listened from another room. Later, after her father's death, she immediately signed up for flying lessons. She became the first woman flying instructor in Tennessee as a member of the WAFS (Women Auxiliary Ferrying Squadron). This led her to Andrews Flying Service in Honolulu, Hawaii, in 1941.

On December 7th, 1941, she was flying with a student when suddenly she saw an immense incoming flight of planes. When the fog lifted, she could see the big red circles on the wings and fuselage and a steady stream of bullets coming from their guns. Black smoke was rising from the ships docked below. Some were able to swim to shore from the wreckage, but many sailors lost their lives that day including those still entombed on the Arizona.

Cornelia grabbed the controls from the student and while barely avoiding a collision with one of the Japanese planes, made their way to John Rogers Airfield. They ran for shelter to the large hanger, feeling lucky to be alive. As the planes continued to bomb, circle repeatedly, strafing anyone in sight, Pearl Harbor was destroyed. War was declared on Japan.

Many didn't believe Cornelia's story about seeing the attack from the air. Seeing the holes in her plane convinced them her story was true.

As a WASP (Women Airforce Service Pilots) in 1943, Cornelia was the first woman pilot killed in active duty. In March, a group of WASPs were ferrying a group of training aircraft from Long Beach, California, to Dallas Love Field in Texas. Somewhere in the last leg of the journey, Cornelia's plane collided with one of the other planes. She lost part of a wing causing her to plunge to her death. She was twenty-four years old. A few weeks before her death, she had unknowingly written her own epitaph: "I am grateful that my one talent, flying, was useful to my country".

Cornelia's story was provided to the author by the National WWII Museum New Orleans.

THE ROSIES

Dorothy Martus

28

Beulah McAlister

I was born in Tennessee. When I was one-and-a-half my mother died, and soon after I lost my father. My grandparents took me to their home in Kentucky and raised me. I graduated in 1941. My boyfriend and I got married and moved to Detroit. Dick was drafted nine months later, and I went to work. Jobs were plentiful. I was hired as a riveter at the Hudson Motor Car Company. We never knew what we were working on. We thought it was airplane wings, and a supervisor verified it. He said, "Don't tell anyone".

"Loose lips sink ships" was everywhere, reminding us the enemy was listening.

I worked ten hours a day, six days a week. I was paid 85 cents an hour. We started wearing slacks. Slacks for women didn't become common for several years though. Our hair had to be tied up, so we wore men's big, red handkerchiefs for that.

I worked at that job for two years before I quit to be with my husband in Texas for a few weeks before he was to be shipped out. When it was time for him to leave, I took our baby and went to Kentucky to my grandparents' home for the duration of the war.

29

Dorothy Martus

I was born in Deerfield Township, Michigan, in 1923. I had one sister and a brother. My dad was a potato farmer. I was his "righthand man", driving the horses, helping in the many ways kids do when they live on a farm.

When I graduated, I wanted a job to make money. I tried several local jobs but was not satisfied. My sister and her husband and several other relatives and friends had gone to the Willow Run Plant in Ypsilanti to build planes. I got a job there too. I lived with my sister. For a few days, some were nervous about coming to work because there were riots in nearby Detroit. A black friend was allowed to sleep in a plane for he was afraid to walk home.

My job here was to attach antennas to the nose of the planes. It was good we were now wearing slacks because of the way we had to crawl around those planes.

I worked a regular eight-hour shift, but the shift rotated every month. Sometimes our weekends were shorter because of it; other days it didn't matter.

I wanted to go home to see my boyfriend one weekend. Of course, I had no car. I took a train from Ypsilanti to Detroit, another from Detroit to Pontiac, and from Pontiac to city limits I took a jitney. Then I hitchhiked. A fellow who lived near us took me the rest of the way home.

After one-and-a-half years of being a Rosie, I quit and went home to get married. We had ten children. I was an involved, very busy mother and wife.

30

Elizabeth (Betty) McInally

I am Elizabeth McInally. I was born in Traverse City in 1925. My dad was a lumberman. I had one brother who served in the Army. My mom died when I was five or six years old. Then I was sent to live with an uncle who already had ten kids but opened their home and heart to me. I went to school while there, walking three miles each way, until I graduated eighth grade.

After that I went across the street to stay with my step-grandma who lived alone. I didn't go on to high school for grandma needed my help. I stayed there until I was sixteen. A friend told me to come to Detroit for she had a job for me and a place to stay. I worked as a babysitter until I was 18 when the war was on, and I went to work at Packards. We made engines for planes. My particular job was taking a cart to the supply room and filling it with parts for the riveters. I worked a regular forty-hour shift. Since my expenses were small, I was able to buy a war bond each payday.

One of the plant guards stopped one day and asked me for a date. I reluctantly said, "Yes". However, I decided I didn't want to go with him. I waited until I thought he had gone, and a man came up to me and asked if I had a date. I said I did have but I dodged him. He said, "No you didn't. It was me". Without his uniform, I didn't recognize him. He left.

I met my future husband when he came to visit someone else where I was staying. We were married two or three years later. I had worked in Detroit two years. My husband worked in Detroit, but when his company moved to North Branch, we moved there too. We had eleven children. When the oldest was sixteen and the youngest four months old, my husband died. There were no organizations to help then, and my church didn't help, so it was a real struggle to care for the family alone. My mother and sister were gone, so it was tough.

Six years later, a bachelor with no kids came along. He loved the kids and was such a good person. We married. He died nine years later, and once again, I was alone. The children were older then, so I could go to work to support us.

Being unable to care for myself, I am now living at Stonegate Retirement Home in Lapeer, Michigan.

OTHER WAR EFFORTS

Bob Hope with a group of Navy WAVES (Women Accepted
for Volunteer Emergency Service)
National World War II Museum

31

A Jewish Voice For Veterans ~ A Veteran's Voice For Jews

The Jewish War Veterans of the USA (JWV) are proud to say they are the longest running veterans service organization out there. They were founded in 1896 by a group of 63 Jewish veterans from the Civil War after a series of anti-Semitic comments about the lack of Jewish service in the Civil War. Since then, the JWV has been working hard to be the voice of American Jewry in the veteran community.

However, they have been up to much more than fighting against anti-Semitism since 1896. In World War I they were essential to establishing the Jewish chaplaincy within the military. They also were responsible for getting grave markers in veterans' cemeteries such as the Star of David. At the rise of the 3rd Reich, they led a huge protest march and boycott of Nazi Germany. In 1938, they led a protest that got Nazi leaders in America deported from America.

In World War II, they fought for Jewish services to be conducted on the battlefield and packages to be sent to our troops from Jewish communities. Racial and religious protections were put into the 1944 GI Bill which allowed Jewish and other minorities to receive benefits to lift them out of poverty.

During the Cold War years, the JWV fought the Ku Klux Klan and John Birch Society and McCarthyism where Jewish American troops were being accused or let go because of their Eastern European upbringing. Their work in the 1960's eventually led to thousands of Soviet Jews being freed from the Eastern Bloc.

The JWV continues to fight injustices that creep into the lives of these people such as their medals being withheld and correcting rumors about the Jewish not doing their part in the fighting it took to win the second world war.

In the past 125 years, they have fought many battles so that the Jewish community can enjoy the same advantages in life as the Gentiles.

32

Tuskegee Airmen

At the beginning of the war, African Americans were not allowed in pilot training. Due to pressure by Eleanor Roosevelt, Civil Rights Groups, the Black press, and others, the U.S. Army Air Corps was told to open its pilot training to Negroes. They were to be a totally segregated squadron with all Black ground staff in Tuskegee, Alabama. These men were the first aviators in the U.S. Army Air Corps, a precursor of the U.S. Air Force.

This 99th Fighter Squadron flew more than 15,000 individual sorties. Their impressive performance earned them more than 150 Distinguished Flying Crosses and helped to encourage the eventual integration of the U.S. Armed Forces.

These pilots escorted American bombers as they flew over Italy. As escorts, flying P47s and later P51s, they were responsible for protecting larger bombers from German fighter planes.

OUR HEROES NEXT DOOR | 113

Stone pillar at the entrance of the Tuskegee Airmen National
Historic Site Alabama, 2019.
iStock photo.

33

Japanese Americans in World War II Combat

The 101st unit joined the 442nd Regimental Combat Team that was made up of Nisei, American-born Japanese. Many were drafted from the detention camps out west. They were deployed to Europe, fighting in eight major campaigns in France and Italy. Liberating Dachau Concentration Camp brought memories of their families still held in the detention camps back home in the states.

The 442nd is remembered today for their brave actions in World War II. Despite the odds, the small 442nd's actions distinguished them as the most decorated unit of its size and length of service in the history of the U.S. military. Their motto was "Go For Broke".

34

Prisoner of War Camps in 1943

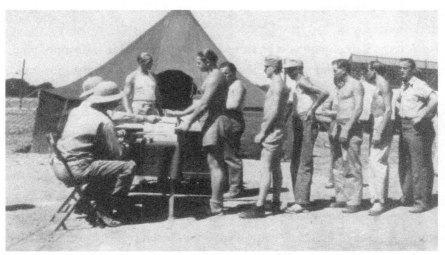

German prisoners of war at a camp near Owosso, Michigan

As prisoners of war from Europe, mainly Italy and Germany, began arriving in the United States, it soon was decided Michigan was a place of major need. There was demand for labor in all the factories. Agriculture was an important factor also. This choice was made over the southern area which had advantages of better climate with lower expenses.

The prisoners were housed in barracks. It was thought it was okay to choose men for each barrack randomly. However, it was soon learned that choosing those mixing from democratic areas and those from areas of a warring atmosphere like Nazism wouldn't live together peaceably. This was seen in the camps selecting program. Men showing too much aggression towards others were transferred to a camp set aside for them.

Definite rules were established for the prisoners as well as for the Americans. Both were to avoid close relations with each other. The Americans were constantly reminded that these men were the enemy even though they didn't act like it. President Eisenhower demanded that all be treated as the Geneva Convention of 1929 commands – fairly and humanely.

A large percentage was anxious to surrender and just dropped their weapons and raised their hands. They were tired of fighting in cold, wet weather with inadequate food, weapons, and equipment. Morale rose as they realized they had a chance of seeing their homes again. They were treated humanely. Food was scarce, but they were given what could be obtained locally mostly. Overall, it was much better than our Americans endured in foreign camps. Our boys who came home came with damaged or missing limbs and mental problems.

The prisoners, especially those who worked closely with the Americans, developed lifetime relationships with each other. Some returned to America after the war to make this their permanent home. They brought their families here or married American girls. Some were lifetime pen pals.

The work that these men did in the absence of our own men was tremendous. The lumber industry in the upper peninsula alone was worth hundreds of thousands of dollars. Factories such as the baby-food factory in Owosso hired prisoners. Two American girls who worked there became good "friends" with two of the men. This friendship led to the girls helping the men escape. The departure led to only about twenty-four hours of freedom before they were captured. One of the girls spent a year in prison for the escapade, the other one less. The story made international news.

It was hard to feel hatred towards these men because they wanted to be here, and few caused trouble. When they went out for a day's work, they were given two slices of bread with a slice of meat or cheese. Those going to work on farms looked forward to it and hoped for return trips. Farm wives usually fed the prisoners well. The closeness resulted in friendships that lasted a long time.

The prisoners could wear their own uniform if it was in good shape. If they left camp, they had to wear their green or blue denim uniform with POW written on the back. Americans treated the men kindly, and the prisoners responded favorably. It made life better for all.

A local German veteran came here from a camp program in North Africa. He learned English on his own and helped the camp with interpreting. This awarded him some special privileges.

Since these camps were made up of men from different backgrounds, one might find spare time was used in many ways such as teams playing sports, card games, classical music, painting or carving, any form of busyness you might find in any community.

The war moved on and reports came of a cease fire. Prisoners wondered if it they were false rumors. Old thoughts of loyalty to their own country erupted and fights among the men occurred. The war did cease, but the camps were not emptied until a year later. Some believed they weren't sent home sooner because their labor was still needed. All sorts of transportation were needed to get these men to the ships, and they were needed to get our men and women home too. Some of the men would have liked to stay here permanently, but military law forbade it. Some had no home to go to. Cash was no problem for them for they had jobs that paid them well. There were millions of military and non-military staff thousands of miles from home waiting for their turn to travel. This was a monumental task, especially in areas where streets, roads, buildings, railroads, etc. were destroyed.

Since 75-80 years have passed from the time these barracks were needed, there is little or no evidence that they existed. Their stories remain hidden in the hearts of those who lived them and perhaps their families.

35

War Brings Changes At Home

1. The government asked for a voluntary 35 mph speed limit to save gas.
2. Ration books were issued to each person. There were stamps for butter, sugar, coffee, gasoline, fuel oil, and shoes. Stamp #17 in Book 4 was for a pair of shoes through Sears Roebuck. There was a very stiff penalty for ration-book fraud.
3. Coffee was scarce because it had to be shipped in. Soon people found they could stretch its use by mixing it with chicory.
4. Margarine was developed because butter was scarce. At first it came in clear plastic bags about 7 inches square. In the corner was a yellow capsule. We squeezed and broke the capsule, working it into the white margarine until it was yellow. Then we put it into a bowl.
5. As kids, we missed bubble gum. The rubber in it came from Asia. After Pearl Harbor, many substitutes had to be found for tires and other things. A synthetic tire was developed and later they were made of nylon.
6. Nylon had been on the research table for some time and was now being used for many things: parachutes, clothing, things

too numerous to count. Nylon hose was a biggie. Until this time, women wore cotton hose or silk hose. Silk was no longer available. Women's hose had a seam up the back and a slight nick soon became a run. Women sometimes left their hose at home and drew a line up the back of their legs with their eyebrow pencil to look like they had on hose.

7. Pennies were not made of copper. They were made of steel and called "steelies".

8. Kids collected metal and milk weed fluff. The fluff was used in life vests.

9. There were few domestic airlines. Travel was by bus, train, or car. A lot of hitchhiking was done. It was safe.

Author's ration book

36

Author's World War II Memories

Through three generations, my family has been involved in all four branches of the military. As an eleven-year-old, I heard the broadcast of the attack on Pearl Harbor. The next day I heard President Roosevelt's "This Day Will Go Down in Infamy" speech. Then my three uncles enlisted. Mom went to work in a factory which made bombs. My dad worked at building planes. I started my World War II albums, and my interest in the war took off.

Later in life I visited the Holocaust Museum in Farmington Hills, Michigan. There I was encouraged by one of the survivor speakers to put their stories in a book. *Coffee Grounds and Potato-Peeling Pancakes* was the outcome of that connection.

Then my interest was jolted again several years later when I met Bonnie Koning and the "Veterans Esteem Team". This book, *Our Heroes Next Door*, was the result of that future relationship. The book is a collection of the stories the veterans, Rosies, and a WAC related to me about their World War II experiences. I gained a lot of friendships and learned a lot of history.

Family members included in this journey include:

Charles Anderson

Army: 1. **Husband, Marvin Bigelow** – occupation of Japan, paratrooper, manager of base commissary, four years of service; 2. **Brother, Charles Anderson** – occupation of Japan, paratrooper, two years of service; 3. **Uncle, Earl Vaught** – extensive battles with General Eisenhauer, tank mechanic, liberation of concentration camp Nordhausen, Germany – four and one-half years of service.

Marines: **Uncle, Omer Vaught** – based on USS Lexington, battles on many islands with fierce battles in the South Pacific including Iwo Jima, Leyte, Tokyo, Wake Island, Okinawa, and Philippine Islands, and Lexington Air Group poised for strike on Tokyo at end of the war.

Navy: **Uncle, Chester Vaught** – very limited time in service due to asthma.

Uncle Earl's unit liberated the
Nordhausen Camp

Air Force: 1. **Cousin, Patrick King** – started military career as a mechanic crew chief on F-22 planes. Next, he was trained as a meteorologist and has continued in that area of work until now. He presently is in a classified program. He plans to reach retirement within a few months; 2. **Nephew, Timothy Serchett** – went to Korea, Egypt, Kuwait, and Turkey to work on missiles, bombs, and aircraft ammunitions, maintenance supervisor for C5 aircraft (largest aircraft we had at the time). After World War II, Russians built "The Wall" during the "Cold War" which ended 1989-1990. He witnessed the historical event of it coming down – twenty-three years of service.

The author received this postcard in the
mail from Uncle Chester C. Vaught in
1943.

3. **Nephew, Dennis King** – first assignment was as a Security Force Specialist at NATP Base Incirlik, Turkey. Coming back to the USA, he trained to be an Air Traffic Controller where he advanced to become chief controller in both tower and radar approach facilities. With career broadening, he completed training as a first sergeant in the 22nd Air Refueling Squadron at Mountain Home Air Force Base in Idaho. After this, Dennis was selected for reassignment to the Air Force Flight Standards Agency at Andrews Air Force Base, Maryland. As a senior master sergeant, he completed his career at AFFSA in the position of ASAF Chief Air Traffic Control Evaluations. In his twenty-one years of service, Dennis' assignments took him to Texas, Turkey, Michigan, Japan, and Idaho.

The Vaught uncles: Earl, Omer, and Chester

Many meetings are required to sell books. As I go to schools, libraries, historical societies, and other organizations, I get to relive the stories these veterans have shared. The teacher of the Quest program at North Branch Schools also invites me to speak when he is teaching the world history section of World War II.

All of this is a challenge for me as a ninety-one-year-old, but when something like this is so much a part of your life, God provides the stamina and you just keep going.

Helen O. Bigelow

P.S. All profits from book sales will go to benefit veteran programs.

Appreciation from Veterans Esteem Team

The Veterans Esteem Team is a group of students and volunteers who promote awareness and appreciation for military veterans of the U.S. This organization began in 2015 when some local students began researching what was being done locally for our veterans. The results were astounding. There were large gaps in providing for the needs of these men and women.

One group of veterans that seemed to have the greatest needs was the World War II veterans. Many live alone and do not travel outside their homes very often. While working with this "greatest generation", a golden opportunity appeared. There were stories that they shared from the many areas of the world where they served. This historical treasure had been hidden from most people. What a privilege it was to hear the stories first-hand from these warriors! Amazingly, while all of these veterans are in their 90's, most could clearly recollect their special moments and years during World War II. For some, it meant recalling some difficult experiences, and we were thankful to share in their tears as well as their joys.

When a local author, Helen Bigelow, approached us about the possibility of recording these stories in a new book she was willing to write, it seemed like a dream come true. While our organization is a student group, it seemed like the perfect opportunity to record history for our current members, future student team members, and the

128 | *Appreciation from Veterans Esteem Team*

community. Being in the 90's herself, Helen, as a girl of 11 years, recalls her uncles being in World War II. She shared her multiple scrap books she has kept showing her concern for the war at a young age. She has made every effort to meet with our local World War II heroes to accurately record their stories. What a legacy she has created by taking on this task!

As the Veterans Esteem Team, our deepest thanks go to our local heroes for sharing their heartfelt stories. They will forever be in our hearts. A special appreciation goes to Helen Bigelow for taking on the task of interviewing no matter where or when it would take her. Her dedication to our heroes and history will forever be a part of us and our community.

Bonnie Koning

Helen Bigelow is a retired schoolteacher and counselor who has lived a busy life including her volunteer work and traveling. Through her travels, she developed long-term friendships with people worldwide. During the 1970's and 80's, she and her husband hosted foreign exchange students from Brazil and Mexico. Many of those students remain part of Helen's extended family. In the meantime, she has been an active member of her church and has enjoyed playing cards and tending to her flower gardens. Helen and her family have been active strawberry growers for 54 years. They also were active in their horticulture business for many years. They have been residents of the rural North Branch area for nearly sixty years.

This is the second book she has written due to her passion with World War II history. Her first book, *Coffee Grounds and Potato-Peeling Pancakes* was written due to her relationship with a Jewish woman survivor of the Holocaust. She maintains her relationship with those who shared their stories with her in that book. Helen has been a friend and mentor to many including those who she interviewed in this book.

CPSIA information can be obtained
at www.ICGtesting.com
Printed in the USA
JSHW021932240223
38207JS00002B/7